GENIUS RECIPES

FOOD52

# GENIUS RECIPES

## 100 RECIPES THAT WILL CHANGE THE WAY YOU COOK

KRISTEN MIGLORE

PHOTOGRAPHY BY JAMES RANSOM

TEN SPEED PRESS
BERKELEY

# CONTENTS

FOREWORD
Amanda Hesser & Merrill Stubbs / xi

INTRODUCTION / xv

## Breakfast / 1

## Snacks & Drinks / 31

## Soups & Salads / 61

Romaine Hearts with
Caesar Salad Dressing / 63
FROM FRANKIES SPUNTINO

Fresh Fig & Mint Salad / 64
FROM RICHARD OLNEY

"Use a Spoon" Chopped Salad / 67
FROM MICHEL NISCHAN

Radicchio Salad with
Manchego Vinaigrette / 68
FROM TORO BRAVO

*Garlic-Scented Tomato Salad / 68*
FROM MARCELLA HAZAN

Warm Squash & Chickpea Salad
with Tahini / 70
FROM MORO

Kale Salad / 74
FROM NORTHERN SPY FOOD CO.

Green Peach Salad / 77
FROM CROOK'S CORNER

Red Salad / 79
FROM FERGUS HENDERSON

Wild & White Rice Salad / 80
FROM VIANA LA PLACE & EVAN KLEIMAN

Roasted Carrot & Avocado Salad
with Crunchy Seeds / 83
FROM ABC KITCHEN

Chickpea Stew with Saffron,
Yogurt & Garlic / 84
FROM HEIDI SWANSON

Spicy Tomato Soup / 87
FROM BARBARA LYNCH

Cauliflower Soup / 88
FROM PAUL BERTOLLI

Potato Soup with Fried Almonds / 91
FROM ANYA VON BREMZEN

*Cheese Brodo / 92*
FROM NATE APPLEMAN

*Lemon Salt / 92*
FROM PATRICIA WELLS

*Chicken Stock / 92*
FROM TOM COLICCHIO

*Red Wine Vinaigrette / 92*
FROM MOLLY WIZENBERG & BRANDON PETTIT

## Meaty Mains / 95

Salt-Baked Herbed Salmon with
Red Onion-Caper Vinaigrette / 97
FROM CORY SCHREIBER

Shrimp Grits / 98
FROM EDNA LEWIS & SCOTT PEACOCK

Crispy-Skinned Fish / 101
FROM LE BERNARDIN

Rosemary-Brined Buttermilk
Fried Chicken / 102
FROM MICHAEL RUHLMAN

Simplest Roast Chicken / 106
FROM BARBARA KAFKA

Chicken Thighs with Lemon / 108
FROM CANAL HOUSE

Dry-Brined Turkey (a.k.a. The Judy Bird) / 111
FROM RUSS PARSONS

*Cranberry Sauce / 112*
FROM DANIEL HUMM

Onion Carbonara / 115
FROM MICHEL RICHARD

Sticky Balsamic Ribs / 119
FROM IAN KNAUER

Carnitas / 120
FROM DIANA KENNEDY

Grilled Pork Burgers / 122
FROM SUZANNE GOIN

Brisket of Beef / 127
FROM NACH WAXMAN

Meatballs / 131
FROM RAO'S

Salt-Crusted Beef Tenderloin
Grilled in Cloth (Lomo al Trapo) / 132
FROM STEVEN RAICHLEN

Perfect Pan-Seared Steaks / 137
FROM J. KENJI LÓPEZ-ALT

## Meatless Mains / 139

Cauliflower Steaks / 141
FROM DAN BARBER

Pasta with Yogurt & Caramelized Onions / 144
FROM DIANE KOCHILAS

Mushroom Bourguignon / 147
FROM DEB PERELMAN

*Polenta Facile / 148*
FROM CARLO MIDDIONE

Tomato Sauce with Butter
& Onion / 151
FROM MARCELLA HAZAN

Grilled Pizza / 153
FROM AL FORNO

Ginger Fried Rice / 156
FROM JEAN-GEORGES VONGERICHTEN
& MARK BITTMAN

Spiced Braised Lentils & Tomatoes
with Toasted Coconut / 159
FROM MELISSA CLARK

*Baked Brown Rice / 159*
FROM ALTON BROWN

Pasta with Let-My-Eggplant-Go-Free! Puree / 161
FROM FRANCIS LAM

Kale Panini / 165
FROM ANDREA REUSING

Ship's Biscuit / 166
FROM SALTIE

*Grilled Cheese Sandwiches / 166*
FROM GABRIELLE HAMILTON

Green Lentil Salad / 169
FROM PATRICIA WELLS

Black Pepper Tofu / 170
FROM YOTAM OTTOLENGHI

## Vegetables / 173

Whole Roasted Cauliflower
with Whipped Goat Cheese / 174
FROM ALON SHAYA

Broccoli Cooked Forever / 176
FROM ROY FINAMORE

Garlic Green Beans / 179
FROM PENELOPE CASAS

*Ginger Juice / 179*
FROM MOLLY STEVENS

Balsamic Glazed Beets & Greens / 180
FROM PETER BERLEY

Grilled Chard Stems
with Anchovy Vinaigrette / 183
FROM ANNA KLINGER

Roasted Brussels Sprouts with
Fish Sauce Vinaigrette / 184
FROM MOMOFUKU

Fried Asparagus with Miso Dressing / 188
FROM NOBU MATSUHISA

Ratatouille / 191
FROM ALICE WATERS

Gratin of Zucchini, Rice & Onions
with Cheese / 193
FROM JULIA CHILD

*Grated & Salted Zucchini / 194*
FROM JULIA CHILD

Potato Dominoes / 197
FROM FRANCIS MALLMANN

## Desserts / 199

# Foreword
## Amanda Hesser & Merrill Stubbs

We've cooked thousands of recipes together, and when you cook that much, you begin to develop an eye for the crucial distinctions that make a standout recipe—an exemplar. These are the recipes that inspire you to change how you make a standard dish, that become the recipes you cook for the rest of your life. Nigella Lawson's dense chocolate loaf cake was greater than all the other versions we tried because of the logic-defying amount of water you add to the batter—which makes the cake luxuriously moist, and even better the next day.

These special recipes would crop up from time to time, and after a while we could see they belonged in a category all their own: genius recipes.

And we knew just the person to uncover these gems. We hired Kristen as our first team member when Food52.com was a wee upstart, and her extraordinary talents as a writer, editor, and cook quickly became apparent. More recently, as our executive editor, she has shaped our site's voice and look, recruited other excellent editors, and helped make Food52 a hub for passionate cooks.

In 2011, Kristen debuted her first Genius Recipes post on Food52. It featured the River Café's strawberry sorbet (page 200), into which you blend a whole lemon, skin and all. The column immediately became a hit. With tireless curiosity and sly wit, Kristen has introduced us to some of the best recipes from such cooking luminaries as Marcella Hazan, Eric Ripert, Alice Waters, Nigella Lawson, James Beard, Patricia Wells, Craig Claiborne, Martha Stewart, Fergus Henderson, April Bloomfield, Yotam Ottolenghi, and Julia Child, to name just a few.

She has discovered genius recipes from many lesser-known authors and chefs, as well. For Kristen, no stone goes unturned. She's an indefatigable researcher and perfectionist who will test and retest recipes not only to make sure they work exactly as written, but to assess whether or not they're truly genius. She rejected many a recipe that we couldn't find fault with.

Along the way, Kristen has added her own touches of genius. With a strange but delicious caramelized white chocolate recipe (page 230), she discovered that you can use it as an ice cream topping in the vein of Magic Shell. (She also styled the recipes for all of the photos in this book.)

We've become avid fans of her column ourselves. After Kristen wrote about Roy Finamore's broccoli cooked forever (page 176), in which you simmer broccoli and garlic in oil for seemingly days, in essence making a confit with them, Merrill made it so often that she began applying the technique to all species of vegetables from carrots to parsnips to cauliflower. Likewise, Amanda will now only make the genius guacamole by Roberto Santibañez (page 45) from his book *Truly Mexican* for which you crush white onion, cilantro, and salt to a paste and very gently fold in the avocado so as not to smush it, an approach that produces a guacamole that's brighter, more aromatic, and somehow more delicate than any other. The recipe's tiny details have a huge payoff. And that is the brilliant and rewarding principle behind all of the genius recipes in this book.

# Introduction

*Genius recipes surprise us and make us rethink cooking tropes. They're handed down by luminaries of the food world and become their legacies. They get us talking and change the way we cook. And, once we've folded them into our repertoires, they make us feel pretty genius too.*

This is how I framed Genius Recipes when I launched it as a weekly column on Food52 in June 2011. In the years since, the definition really hasn't changed: These recipes are about reworking what we've been taught and skipping past all the canonical versions to a smarter way.

For example, if you were to look to a classical text or cooking class, you'd probably think you'd need to truss and flip and baste a chicken as you're roasting it. And there's nothing necessarily wrong with any of that—you will probably get a good dinner out of the exercise. But Barbara Kafka, in writing the cookbook *Roasting: A Simple Art* in 1995, perfected roasting *everything*, from mackerel to turkeys to cucumbers. She puts chicken in the oven, legs akimbo, at a raging 500°F (260°C), then hardly touches it. Hers is the juiciest roast chicken I've tasted, and has the crispiest skin, without fussing—so why would you?

This book is full of happy discoveries like this roast chicken (page 106), drawn from the experience of the best cookbook authors, chefs, and bloggers around. No one cook could have taught us so much. From historic voices in food like Marcella Hazan, Julia Child, and James Beard to modern giants like Ignacio Mattos and Kim Boyce, we've learned that making something better doesn't mean doing more work—and oftentimes, it means doing less. If you look to the people who've spent their careers tinkering with these dishes, they'll often show you a better way to make them.

Here in this collection are more than one hundred of the most surprising and essential genius recipes. Some are greatest hits from the column that keep inspiring new conversations and winning new fans. I also dug up a bunch more recipes, like Marion Cunningham's famous yeasted overnight waffles (page 29) and Dorie Greenspan's apple cake with more apples than cake (page 221), to stock our kitchens and keep us cooking and talking. You'll also find new tips and variations and a good number of mini-recipes alongside the full-length ones. These genius ideas were simple enough to distill into a paragraph or two and made the collection whole. My hope is that this book, held all together, can act as an alternative kitchen education of sorts.

Some of the recipes are already legends: If you've been reading about food for a while, you've probably already heard of the tomato sauce with butter and onion (page 151), the no-knead bread (page 39), the one-ingredient ice cream (page 200). I love sharing these on Food52, because it seems everyone has an opinion and a good story to tell.

A handful of others are tricks I stumbled across myself: The oddball ingredient I saw when I trailed in the kitchen at Le Bernardin (page 101). The simple carnitas I found in an old Diana Kennedy cookbook when I was missing the burritos at home in California (page 120). The winning ratatouille after I tested four in a day (page 191). The dessert served at the James Beard Awards that Melissa Clark posted on Instagram (page 203)—watch out, world: I'm paying attention!

But if we had to rely on me, Genius Recipes would have been a nice little series that would have petered out long ago—and it surely wouldn't have evolved into a book. I'd hoped I would have help finding the gems, since the spirit of better cooking through community has always driven Food52. But I couldn't have known that the tips would just keep coming—that the majority of the recipes I would gather, and the most unexpectedly brilliant ones, would come from emails and tweets and conversations with the Food52 community, fellow staffers, and other writers, editors, and friends.

I wouldn't have looked twice at a soup made of cauliflower, an onion, and a whole lot of water (page 88). And broccoli cooked forever is almost daring you not to (page 176). But cooks from Food52 said these were worthy of genius status, and they were right. Genius Recipes is proof of the power of crowd-sourcing and curation, but also of listening and trusting other cooks. Even though many of these recipes have been around for years, some for decades, only now can we gather and share them so quickly.

I hope you will use the recipes in a number of ways. Some may become formulas (I don't make roast chicken or guacamole or oatmeal any other way anymore). But others, I hope, will be jumping-off points. Maybe you'll make the kale panini just as written (page 165), then next time you'll use collards or whatever greens you have, or start making just the quick pickled peppers to keep around. As soon as you make the olive oil and maple granola (page 15) once, if you're like the legions of commenters on Food52, you'll start tweaking it and making it your own.

Please do, and the next time you discover something genius, let me know.

# Breakfast

# Fried Eggs with Wine Vinegar

## FROM ROGER VERGÉ

Egg yolk needs something to play against—a spicy sauce to snake through, a buttered piece of toast, crisp potatoes, salty meats. Here's another, a simpler and perhaps better mate for egg yolk than any of these: vinegar. It might not sound as welcome at 9 a.m. as butter or maple—and I know people are stubborn about their fried eggs—but a measured shot of vinegar is surprisingly perfect at breakfast. Just think about hot sauce: We don't reach for it because it's like ketchup, but rather because it's like vinegar.

Roger Vergé, one of the forefathers of nouvelle cuisine, knows this. The richness of yolk is tempered best by sitting next to something tart and cleansing—the balance of soft and sharp acting like a good vinaigrette.

While Vergé is quite specific about his eggs, his technique can be applied to your favorite fried egg method, whatever it may be. Just splash a couple tablespoons of vinegar into the hot, still-buttery pan as soon as the eggs come out. Let it reduce by half, then spill the resulting syrup over your eggs. As you bite in, the brightness will startle you, then feel strangely familiar and comforting. If you need to ease in, you could swirl in some butter at the end with the vinegar, much like mounting a proper pan sauce. But you'll see it's not necessary once the yolk is unleashed.

## Serves 2

4 large eggs (6 if you enjoy them as much as Vergé does)
2 tablespoons butter
¼ cup (60ml) good-quality wine vinegar
Salt and freshly ground black pepper

1 Break 2 or 3 eggs, according to your appetite, into a bowl, taking care not to break the yolks. Heat 1 tablespoon of the butter in a 6-inch (15cm) frying pan, preferably nonstick, and when it turns golden, slip in the eggs very carefully. Cook, puncturing any air bubbles that form in the egg whites with a fork. Don't worry if the eggs go crisp and golden round the edge. When they are cooked the way you like them, season with salt and freshly ground pepper and slide onto a heated plate.

2 Pour 2 tablespoons of the vinegar into the pan. Allow to reduce by half and pour over the eggs.

3 Wipe out the pan with a cloth or paper towel and repeat the process with the remaining eggs, butter, and vinegar.

---

"This is a controversial recipe. Some people swear that the butter should not be allowed to color; others cook the whites first on their own and then slide the yolks on top (having first salted the whites to prevent the yolks from being marked). Each way has its point, but I have given the recipe I make for myself and my friends. Fried eggs cooked in this way are, incidentally, among the most irresistible of all dishes. Many is the time that I have suddenly had a longing for three fried eggs—usually after midnight, when I am among friends and guests who have finished dinner and are mulling away the evening with a liqueur. The sight of the eggs cooking is too much for them all, and they always end up by joining me. I know few dishes so powerful!" —R. V.

# Chocolate Muscovado Banana Cake

FROM NIGEL SLATER

Breakfast pastries are essentially pie, scones might as well be cookies, and—let's face it—banana bread is really just cake. At least this breakfast cake has a whole lot of banana in it.

Cookbook author and *Observer* columnist Nigel Slater shows us that to make the best cake, we need to treat it as such. Unlike most banana bread recipes that call for simply stirring in oil or melted butter, his tells us to cream butter and sugar to give it loft and a sturdy, crunchy crust. He also uses muscovado (or dark brown sugar) to twist a pleasant, standard sweetness into a deep caramel thrum, which, rather than obscuring the banana flavor, gets it all riled up (think bananas Foster). With all that banana and moist, molasses-rich sugar, the cake is even better on days two and three.

I stand by the assertion that this is no less healthy, and no less breakfast, than any other banana bread. Think of this as the treat you bring to the office, on road trips, or for holiday brunch—or, if you're like me, as a sensible alternative to the Danish at the coffee shop.

**GENIUS TIP**

If you're coming up shy on the banana, you can scrape the insides of the peels for a bit more matter. It might look a little stringy, but break it up enough and it's as good as any banana, melting softly into the crumb.

### Makes 1 loaf cake

2 cups (250g) all-purpose flour

2 teaspoons baking powder

½ cup (125g) butter, softened

1 cup plus 1 tablespoon (235g) muscovado sugar

14 ounces (400g) ripe bananas (peeled weight), about 3 medium bananas

1 teaspoon pure vanilla extract

2 large eggs

3½ ounces (100g) dark chocolate

1 Preheat the oven to 350°F (180°C). You will need a nonstick loaf pan approximately 9½ by 5 by 3 inches (24 by 12 by 8cm) deep, lined with parchment paper. Sift the flour and baking powder together.

2 Using an electric mixer, cream the butter and sugar together till light, fluffy, and pale coffee colored.

3 Put the bananas in a bowl and mash them with a fork. The mixture should be lumpy rather than crushed to a puree. Stir in the vanilla. Beat the eggs lightly with a fork, then beat them into the butter and sugar mixture. Introduce a spoonful of the measured flour at any sign of curdling. Chop the chocolate into small pieces—about the size of fine gravel—and fold them and the bananas into the butter and sugar mixture. Gently fold in the flour and baking powder.

4 Scrape the mixture into the lined loaf pan and bake for about 50 minutes, or until a metal skewer inserted into the center of the cake comes out moist but clean. If there is any sign of wet cake batter, return the cake to the oven for a few more minutes, covering the surface with foil. Leave the cake in its pan to settle for 15 minutes or so, then loosen the sides with a thin spatula and carefully lift out of the pan with the parchment paper liner. Leave to cool a little longer, then carefully peel off the paper. Serve cool, in thick slices.

# Touch-of-Grace Biscuits

FROM SHIRLEY CORRIHER

The answer to dry, dense biscuits? Make them wet. Really, really wet. Because if you take a suspiciously moist batter and put it in a hot oven, you get steam, and your biscuits puff up hot and dewy inside. *Bakewise* author Shirley Corriher teaches us how to pull it off: After pinching together the dry ingredients with a bit of shortening (or butter or lard, for you purists), you stir in cream and buttermilk until it looks like cottage cheese. "It should be a wet mess," Corriher says. So even if it's humid or your spooned-and-leveled cups of flour were more loaded than Corriher's, you'll still be okay—because you just keep pouring and stirring until it looks like something that couldn't possibly stand up and become a biscuit.

What keeps the biscuits from spilling all over is this fun step: You plop your batter (from an ice cream scoop!) into a pie plate full of flour, then toss it around and let the flour fall through your fingers, until you're left with just a lump of dough bound together by a thin skin of flour. Then you roll them into your buttered cake pan, nudging them up against each other, so none has a chance to fall flat. They get steamy, soft middles while the tops and outer edges turn coppery and crisp.

They're squat little puffs you'll want to grab from a basket passed over fried chicken (page 102) or bacon and eggs. Though it's certainly not needed, feel free to spread them with butter (or corn butter, page 8), or pour gravy all over them.

---

## GENIUS TIP

If you can't find self-rising flour, you can swap in 2 cups (250g) of all-purpose flour, 3 teaspoons of baking powder, and 1 teaspoon of salt for the self-rising flour (omitting the rest of the salt in the recipe).

**Makes 12 to 14 biscuits**

Butter for greasing or nonstick cooking spray

2 cups (9 ounces/255g) spooned and leveled self-rising flour (preferably low-protein southern U.S. flour like White Lily)

¼ cup (1.8 ounces/50g) sugar (or less, if you prefer your biscuits less sweet)

½ teaspoon salt

¼ cup (1.6 ounces/45g) shortening

⅔ cup (160ml) heavy cream

1 cup (240ml) buttermilk, or enough for dough to resemble cottage cheese (if you are not using low-protein flour, it will take more than 1 cup)

1 cup (4.5 ounces/125g) all-purpose flour, for shaping

3 tablespoons unsalted butter, melted, for brushing, plus more butter for serving, if desired

1 Preheat the oven to 425°F (220°C) and arrange a shelf slightly below the center of the oven. Butter an 8- or 9-inch (20cm or 23cm) round cake pan or spray with nonstick cooking spray.

2 In a large mixing bowl, stir together the self-rising flour, sugar, and salt. Work the shortening in with your fingers until there are no large lumps. Gently stir in the cream, then some of the buttermilk, until dough resembles cottage cheese. It should be a wet mess—not soup, but it should have the texture of cottage cheese. If you are not using a low-protein flour, this may require considerably more than 1 cup (240ml) of buttermilk.

3 Spread the plain all-purpose flour (not self-rising—it will give a bitter taste to the outside of the biscuits) out on a plate or pie pan. With a medium (2-inch/5cm/#30) ice cream scoop or spoon, place three or four scoops of dough well apart in the flour. Sprinkle flour over each. Flour your hands. Turn a dough ball in the flour to coat, pick it up, and gently shape it into a round, shaking off

CONTINUED

the excess flour as you work. Place this biscuit in the prepared pan. Coat each dough ball in the same way and place each shaped biscuit scrunched up against its neighbor so that the biscuits rise up and don't spread out. Continue scooping and shaping until all the dough is used.

4 Bake until lightly browned, 20 to 25 minutes. Brush with the melted butter. Invert onto one plate, then back onto another. With a knife or spatula, cut quickly between biscuits to make them easy to remove. Serve immediately: "Butter 'em while they're hot."

## One-Ingredient Corn Butter
ADAPTED FROM WHITNEY WRIGHT

This is pure corn, thickened until spreadable and called butter. When she worked at Per Se, Whitney Wright stirred it into a sweet corn risotto—but it can also be spooned on biscuits (pictured opposite), cornbread, muffins, or sandwiches, folded into sautéed spinach, or blended into a milkshake.

Cut the kernels from eight ears of corn (more or less), scraping the juice from the cobs with the back of your knife, too. Juice the kernels (if you have a juicer) or put them in a blender and let it run on the highest speed for about 2 minutes. Once you have a smooth puree, push it through a fine strainer with a rubber spatula.

Heat the strained juice over medium heat in a saucepan, whisking constantly, until the mixture begins to thicken and the frothy bubbles begin to disappear, about 4 minutes. When the mixture is thick and bubbling, whisk and cook for about 30 seconds more. Remove from the heat. Taste it—it should be sweet, smooth, earthy, and buttery. If you want, add a little salt and butter. Makes 3 cups and keeps in the fridge for 3 to 5 days.

# English Porridge

### FROM APRIL BLOOMFIELD

When English chef April Bloomfield's first book, *A Girl and Her Pig,* came out in 2012, it wasn't her famous crispy pig ear salad or lamb burger that really got people talking. It was porridge.

A bowl of steel-cut oats is a chewy, hearty coal miner's breakfast. Made from nubbly, chopped-up whole oat groats, it's a stand-up oatmeal with loads of flavor and texture, but can take a good 30 or 40 minutes to break down and become porridge-like. Rolled oats are the standard weekday alternative—hulled, steamed, and flattened, they make a quick-cooking porridge that runs smooth and doesn't bite back. Can we all agree that both of these can get a bit tiresome midway through the bowl?

Bloomfield negotiates between too much and too little chew with equal parts of both styles of oats, to give us a porridge that's (finally) just right. Cooking them together for just 20 minutes means the steel-cut oats keep their pop while the rolled oats melt around them. She also simmers the oats in half water, half milk—creamy enough to make your breakfast feel rich and loving, without slogging you down—along with what seems like a whole lot of sea salt.

But it won't be too much, because at the end you'll add something sweet and something milky. Or a few spoonfuls of Judy Rodgers's not-too-sweet roasted applesauce (page 12). The oatmeal might also make you think of risotto, and next time you'll want to go savory and try some Parmesan cheese and a runny egg on top instead. However you take yours, this is a simple enough formula that you'll memorize it quickly, and start cooking all your porridge this way.

**Serves 2 or 3**

1½ cups (360ml) whole milk, plus a few generous splashes

1½ teaspoons Maldon or another flaky sea salt (if using finer salt, start with ½ teaspoon and add to taste)

½ cup (50g) rolled oats (not "quick-cooking" or "instant")

½ cup (80g) steel-cut oats

About 2 tablespoons sugar (maple, brown, or white) or maple syrup

1 Combine the 1½ cups milk, 1½ cups (360ml) water, and the salt in a pot (a 2-quart/1.9L pot should do it) and set over high heat. As soon as the liquid comes to a gentle simmer, add both kinds of oats and lower the heat to medium.

2 Cook the oats at a steady simmer, stirring frequently and tweaking the heat as necessary to maintain the simmer, for about 20 minutes. The rolled oats will have turned a bit mushy, while the steel-cut oats will be just tender and pop when you bite them. Turn off the heat. Have a taste. It should be good and salty. Now, add sugar or syrup to your taste (Bloomfield likes her porridge to taste a little salty at first, then fade into sweet): Spoon the porridge into warm bowls and let it sit for a minute. Then carefully pour a little cold milk around the edges of each bowl, so it pools all the way round. Sprinkle a five-fingered pinch of sugar or drizzle syrup in the center of each and let it melt, then serve right away.

# Roasted Applesauce

FROM JUDY RODGERS

No cinnamon, no cloves—this sauce is straight apple.

It comes from Judy Rodgers's *Zuni Café Cookbook* and—as with everything served at her San Francisco restaurant—it's smart and simple, balancing the apples only as needed with small amounts of salt, sugar, and apple cider vinegar. Not only does this quick oven method free you from stewing and stewing applesauce on the stovetop, but it does the magic that roasting always does. All the sugars concentrate, allowing apples to become the best version of themselves. There's just a little bit of butter too, sliced into wafers that melt into bronzed apple tops and a rich sauce.

**Makes about 3 cups (710ml)**

3½ to 4 pounds (1.6 to 1.8kg) apples (Rodgers recommends crisp eating apples, like Sierra Beauties, Braeburns, Pippins, Golden Delicious, or Galas)
Pinch of salt
Up to 2 teaspoons sugar, as needed
About 2 tablespoons unsalted butter
A splash of apple cider vinegar, as needed

1 Preheat oven to 375°F (190°C).

2 Peel, core, and quarter the apples. Toss with a little salt and, unless they are very sweet, a bit of sugar to taste. If they are tart enough to make you squint, add the full measure of sugar. Spread in a shallow baking dish that crowds the apples in a single layer. Drape with slivers of the butter, cover tightly with a lid or aluminum foil, and bake until the apples start to soften, 15 to 30 minutes, depending on your apples.

3 Uncover, raise the heat to 500°F (260°C), and return the pan to the oven. Leave the apples to dry out and color slightly, about 10 minutes.

4 When the tips of the apples have become golden and the fruit is tender, scrape them into a bowl and stir into a chunky "mash." Season with salt and sugar to taste, then consider a splash of apple cider vinegar to brighten the flavor. (Try a drop on a spoonful to see if you like it.) Serve hot or warm.

# Olive Oil & Maple Granola

## FROM NEKISIA DAVIS

If you can stir, you can make this granola. Oats and whatnot go in a bowl (stir), then go into the oven (stir, stir, stir). Granola!

In this granola from Nekisia Davis of Early Bird Foods, olive oil, maple, brown sugar, and salt form a rich, shaggy crust on a wholesome mix of oats, pecans, coconut shards, and various seeds. It leans sweet, but olive oil gives it a savory backbone in a way vegetable oil (the granola standard and a wallflower among oils) never could. Salt keeps it from being cloying.

Both Davis's products and her recipe quickly garnered fans in high places. Martha Stewart was one of the first. Then Melissa Clark. Then Daniel Humm, who not only told *GQ* magazine it was one of his favorite things, but also began producing a version of Davis's recipe in the kitchen of Eleven Madison Park to distribute en masse. Other overachieving restaurants will offer a parting gift of a bundle of chocolate truffles or *pâtes de fruit*, but Humm (a chef known for his sea urchin cappuccino, suckling pig tasting menu, and three Michelin stars) sends every diner home with a jar of low-tech granola smattered with pistachios and dried sour cherries, very much like Early Bird's Jubilee flavor. It's a rare moment of homespun joy in a night of impossible excess—and a testament to how high Davis's recipe has raised the bar.

**GENIUS TIP**

Make like this recipe's growing fan club on Food52: Try it as written, then feel free to vary it endlessly. Experiment with different nuts and seeds or infused olive oils. Stir in chocolate or dried cherries at the end. Add spices. Reduce the sugar or maple, if you like. But whatever you do, don't forget the salt.

**Makes about 7 cups (1.7L)**

3 cups (300g) rolled oats
1 cup (130g) hulled raw pumpkin seeds
1 cup (140g) hulled raw sunflower seeds
1 cup (60g) unsweetened coconut chips
1¼ cups (125g) raw pecans, left whole or coarsely chopped
¾ cup (180ml) pure maple syrup
½ cup (120ml) extra-virgin olive oil
½ cup (110g) packed light brown sugar
Coarse salt

1 Preheat the oven to 300°F (150°C).

2 Put the oats, pumpkin seeds, sunflower seeds, coconut, pecans, maple syrup, olive oil, brown sugar, and 1 teaspoon salt in a large bowl and mix until well combined. Spread the granola mixture in an even layer on a rimmed baking sheet. Bake, stirring every 10 to 15 minutes, until the granola is toasted, about 45 minutes.

3 Remove the granola from the oven and season with more salt to taste. Let cool completely before serving or storing in an airtight container for up to 1 month.

# Poached Scrambled Eggs

FROM DANIEL PATTERSON

You may think there's a finite number of ways—say, six—to cook eggs. Sure, over time we've learned to improve upon the fundamentals, by frying eggs in olive oil or hard-cooking them judiciously rather than boiling their yolks out (see the deviled eggs on page 35). But rarely has an entirely new technique been invented, especially one that doesn't take 40 minutes.

The technique, a hybrid of poaching and scrambling, first came to San Francisco chef and writer Daniel Patterson out of necessity. His fiancé (now wife) made him throw away the Teflon pan he relied upon for scrambling, and he had to get resourceful. He plunged beaten eggs in simmering water and—instead of a potful of loose bits—came up with scrambled eggs. Fluffy, near-instant scrambled eggs.

Adding to their mystique, these scrambled eggs are also made without any fat, yet there's no crusty pan to clean. And, though the recipe is written to serve two, the technique is friendly to scaling and riffing.

In the manner of the 6-minute egg and its variants, it's not such a stretch to call these 40-second eggs, because other than waiting for your water to boil, that's all the time they take. You barely have time to make toast!

Serves 2

4 large eggs
2 tablespoons extra-virgin olive oil (optional)
Fine sea salt and freshly ground black pepper

1 Crack each egg into a medium-mesh sieve (or narrow-slotted spoon), letting the thinner white drain away. Transfer the remaining yolk and white to a small bowl. (If your eggs are very fresh, you can skip this step.) Beat the eggs vigorously with a fork or whisk for 20 seconds.

2 Set a saucepan filled with about 4 inches (10cm) of water over medium heat. Put a strainer in the sink.

When the water is at a low boil, add a few large pinches of salt (if you want the eggs to be well salted, the water should taste like the sea), then stir in a clockwise direction to create a whirlpool. Pour the eggs into the moving water, cover the pot, and count to 20.

3 Turn off the heat and uncover the pot. The eggs should be floating on the surface in ribbons. While holding back the eggs with a spoon, pour off most of the water over the strainer. Gently slide the eggs into the strainer and press them lightly to expel any excess liquid. Tilt the strainer from side to side to release any trapped water (you can even drain the eggs on paper towels, if you like).

4 Scoop the eggs into bowls, drizzle with olive oil, and season with salt and pepper.

---

# Spicy Sauce

ADAPTED FROM TORRISI ITALIAN SPECIALTIES

This is a no-cook hot sauce you can make from the bottles and cans in your pantry year-round, and it will keep for up to 6 months in the fridge. It's the house hot sauce at New York City restaurant Torrisi Italian Specialties and its little sister Parm, where they mix it with sautéed broccoli rabe and spread it on roast turkey sandwiches. Other places to put it: On eggs, fried, scrambled, frittataed. On roast pork and potatoes. On stir-fried greens. On bánh mì or brisket sandwiches. In soups, stews, and pots of beans.

Put 4 ounces (115g) of stemmed B&G hot cherry peppers (or other pickled hot peppers), 2 ounces (60g) of roasted red peppers (jarred is fine), 2 ounces (60g) of crushed tomatoes, ¼ cup (60ml) of olive oil, ¼ teaspoon of crushed red pepper flakes, ¼ teaspoon of dried oregano, and ¼ teaspoon of sugar, plus salt to taste, in a blender or food processor. Blend until smooth, or leave it a little coarse, if you like. Makes 2 cups (475ml). Store in the fridge.

# Yogurt with Toasted Quinoa, Dates & Almonds

## FROM SITKA & SPRUCE

As soon as we heard "complete protein" and "ancient grain" and "gluten-free," quinoa had clinched a place in our brown bag salads, our last-minute dinner sides—even breakfast. But even with all our quinoa literacy, cook times and ratios memorized, many still don't know its greatest trick—that you don't have to boil it at all, and it might be even better if you don't.

Try putting quinoa straight into a skillet and getting it hot. Don't even rinse it first. (That bitter saponin the packages warn about is almost always already washed away during processing anyway.) Your raw quinoa will toast and crackle and smell nutty sooner than you think, so pay attention and pour it off before it goes too far. Now you have a crunchy, raspy garnish—one that's glutenless and ancient and all that, and especially appealing on soft foods like yogurt.

This recipe, from Sitka & Spruce restaurant in Seattle via Amanda Hesser, is a watershed for anyone feeling listless about their yogurt routine. Smear yogurt all over a plate and go at it Pollock-style with your new favorite toasty garnishing grain, nuts, and dried fruit, plus flaky salt (rose salt at Sitka & Spruce, olive salt in Amanda's house), lemon zest, and olive oil.

**Serves 1**

½ tablespoon red quinoa

5 shelled pistachios (raw or salted, either will work), chopped

5 almonds, chopped

6 ounces (170g) whole-milk Greek yogurt

2 medjool dates, pitted and chopped

Pinch of freshly grated lemon zest

Flaky sea salt or other coarse salt—or rose or olive salt, if you can get hold of some

1 to 2 teaspoons best-quality olive oil

1 Preheat the oven to 350°F (175°C).

2 Pour the quinoa into a small sauté pan and place over medium heat. Toast the quinoa for about 2 minutes—it will begin popping when it's toasted, and as soon as it does, pour it into a bowl to cool. Spread the pistachios and almonds in a small baking dish and toast in the oven for about 5 minutes, until they smell nutty and are starting to turn golden. Remove and let cool.

3 Spread the yogurt on a small plate or shallow bowl. Sprinkle on the quinoa, pistachios, almonds, and dates. Fleck with lemon zest and sea salt, and finish with a sprinkling of olive oil.

# Potato Scallion Cakes (Fritterra)

## FROM BERT GREENE

It's not hard to find sweet baking recipes that take advantage of leftover mashed potatoes. But the seasoning complicates matters: You can't put last night's garlic mash into chocolate cake or doughnuts. Or, at least, you shouldn't. Casual bread bakers might work their clumpy potato remnants into flatbreads or country loaves; I bet they've saved the potato cooking water, too. Good for them!

But the rest of us want something simpler, something we'd actually be ready to cook the day after a big feast—something that could work with any family's mashed potato dregs, and make them feel new. Maybe something that would go really well with fried eggs.

I found the solution in cookbook author Bert Greene's *fritterra*—mashed potatoes seasoned and shaped into a cake, then griddled, like you've probably seen before, but with a few smart improvements. "It was a gift from a taxi driver," Greene writes in the recipe's headnote, "who related it in pieces—each time we stopped for a light."

He uses a lot of scallions, but briefly boils them first—a quick extra step that packs in fresh greenness without the bite of raw alliums. And to bind the cakes, Greene uses bread crumbs instead of flour because they don't go gummy when introduced to liquid and are much more forgiving.

These upgrades make for an altogether lighter than average potato cake, and therefore a reasonable post-feast breakfast (or lunch, or dinner).

**Serves 4**

12 whole scallions, bulbs and green tops
2 large eggs, lightly beaten
¼ teaspoon freshly grated nutmeg
½ teaspoon salt (see Genius Tips)
Freshly ground black pepper
¼ cup (15g) fresh bread crumbs
1½ cups (315g) cold mashed potatoes
1 tablespoon olive oil
2 tablespoons vegetable oil

1 Wash and trim the scallions, leaving about 2 inches (5cm) of green stems. Cook in boiling water until tender, about 5 minutes. Drain and finely chop.

2 Place the scallions in a bowl. Add the eggs, nutmeg, salt, pepper to taste, bread crumbs, and mashed potatoes. Mix well.

3 Heat the oils in a large skillet until hot but not smoking. Shape the onion-potato mixture into patties, using 2 rounded tablespoons of the mixture for each patty. Fry about six at a time until golden brown on both sides, 2 or 3 minutes per side. Keep warm while frying the remaining patties. Serve warm.

---

### GENIUS TIPS

Chop the blanched scallions finely, or the cakes will break along scallion fault lines as they fry. And don't be shy with the heat; searing them quickly helps hold the loose batter together—this will keep you from adding too many bread crumbs, which, after a certain point, you will regret.

Depending on what you've already got in your mashed potatoes, you may not need much salt, if any. If you want to be safe, undersalt the mix at first and fry off a tiny test cake, then adjust accordingly.

# Currant Cottage Cheese Pancakes

FROM DEBORAH MADISON

Blueberry pancakes are an iconic breakfast staple, sacred Americana, hazy dream of cold cereal eaters everywhere. But blueberries bleed into tart, black puddles. They sog out pancakes that you were very careful to fluff. And they don't go all that well with maple.

Deborah Madison, who's best known for her vegetarian cookbooks, came up with a better idea in *The Savory Way*, her book dedicated to better home cooking with readily available staples. Tiny dried currants, when plumped up first in hot water (or something stronger) and added generously to a batter, do very good things for a pancake. They thread and disperse seamlessly into the cakes, adding moisture and subtle winey sweetness without spilling out of their skins and flooding the crumb like a sloppy-drunk blueberry would. (For the solution to sloppy-drunk blueberry pie, see page 205.)

Cottage cheese and sour cream give the pancakes even more delicate buoyancy. (Even if you don't understand cottage cheese as a snack, you will understand it in pancake form.) Madison suggests serving with powdered sugar and lemon, but a good smear of salted butter is another fitting option.

**Makes about 20 (3-inch/7.5cm) pancakes**

1 cup (145g) dried currants or raisins
1 cup (225g) cottage cheese, dry-curd if possible
1 cup (230g) sour cream, plus more to serve
5 large eggs
1 teaspoon pure vanilla extract
1 teaspoon grated lemon zest
Several gratings of nutmeg
1 tablespoon sugar
1 cup (125g) unbleached all-purpose flour
1½ teaspoons baking powder
¼ teaspoon salt
Butter, for frying
Confectioners' sugar and lemon, for serving (optional)

1 Unless the currants are soft, cover them with very hot water and set them aside to plump while you make the batter.

2 Whisk the cottage cheese and sour cream together; then beat in the eggs, one at a time. Stir in the vanilla, lemon zest, nutmeg, and sugar; then add the flour, baking powder, and salt. Stir gently to combine without overmixing.

3 Melt a tablespoon of butter in a wide frying pan and, when it's hot, drop in the batter by the spoonful. Cook over medium heat until browned on the bottom, then flip once and cook until lightly colored on the other side.

4 Serve the pancakes with confectioners' sugar and a wedge of lemon, plus extra sour cream if desired.

# Crepes

## FROM KENNY SHOPSIN

Crepes are particular, demanding not just skill and patience, but marksmanship. Crepe batter needs to be rested. It needs to be swirled. The first one, inevitably, is sacrificed—and often many more. Crepes, if you are a perfectionist, require a crepe pan. All of this diligence can result in excellent crepes, but you can produce something remarkably crepe-like without doing any of it.

Instead, do as Kenny Shopsin does at his legendary diner on the Lower East Side of Manhattan: Dunk a big flour tortilla, one side only, into egg and cream. Fry that side in butter while you pour the remaining egg-cream batter on top and spread it around *with your hand*. Flip, then remove and wrap around fruit, or creamy things, or ham and cheese.

It will all feel a little wrong, until you taste your lazy crepes. (Shopsin also invented banana guacamole and mac 'n' cheese pancakes—wrong is his game.) As he wrote in *Eat Me: The Food and Philosophy of Kenny Shopsin*, "Not one person has ever figured out that I wasn't making crepes in the traditional way (of course, I would tell anyone who asked)."

---

**GENIUS TIP**

I often serve these crepes with a simple berry compote. Warm mixed berries (fresh or frozen) in a small pot, sweeten to taste, and sharpen with a squeeze of lemon. If you'd like a thicker compote, you can dissolve a pinch of cornstarch in a little water (or booze), whisk it in, and let it simmer for a minute to thicken.

"This kind of experimentation has a lot to do not only with creativity, but with a lower-than-average repugnance for failure. It goes beyond a willingness to take risks to a willingness to fail miserably." —K.S.

### Makes 1 crepe

1 extra-large egg
1 tablespoon heavy cream
A few drops of pure vanilla extract or rum (optional)
12-inch (30cm) flour tortilla (the thinner the better)
About 1 tablespoon butter, for the griddle

1 Whisk the egg with the cream in a wide bowl. At this point, you could add a few drops of vanilla or a splash of rum if you want to get fancy, but it really doesn't need it. Lay the tortilla in the bowl, push it down to the bottom with your hands, and rotate it so that the entire tortilla is in the bottom of the bowl and the bottom side of the tortilla is throughly covered with the egg mixture.

2 Heat 1 tablespoon of butter (or enough to cover your griddle or a sauté pan large enough to fit the tortilla) over medium-high heat until it begins to bubble. Lift the tortilla out of the liquid and place it, wet side down, on the griddle or pan. Pour the remaining egg-cream mixture on the tortilla and spread it over the tortilla with your fingers. As soon as the underside of the crepe is light brown and mottled, which will be no more than 1 or 2 minutes, flip the crepe over, moving quickly so that the egg mixture doesn't slide off (Shopsin uses his fingers but you can use whatever tool works best for you). Cook the crepe for about 1 more minute on the other side, until it is mottled. Now your crepe is done. You just have to fill it and fold it. You can fill it with anything you like. Shopsin's has all kinds of filling for crepes, sweet and savory, but they are also good with just sugar sprinkled on top.

# Raised Waffles

## FROM MARION CUNNINGHAM

Getting a jumpstart on your waffle batter the night before breakfast isn't just clever time management, and it isn't a questionable shortcut—it will actually get you a better waffle. This one, from Marion Cunningham, the champion of home cooking who revived the Fannie Farmer books in the 1970s, is the only overnight waffle recipe you need to know.

In the same way that long-risen breads taste richer and more of themselves (like Jim Lahey's classic no-knead bread, page 39), a yeasted waffle batter will taste like what a real waffle ought to be, and—in case there was any doubt—confirm that mixes from boxes are a sham.

Stirring together a few ingredients before bed and adding a couple more in the morning is no more difficult than following the back of a box—possibly even easier because you're not trying to tear open a plastic bag full of powder before coffee.

But time management justifications, however true, are almost irrelevant. This waffle will be delicate and crisp at the surface and almost pudding-soft inside, with a yeasty, savory tang that goes down well with maple.

---

### GENIUS TIPS

The batter keeps (and improves) for several days in the fridge, if you want to get even more ahead.

You could also try them with one-third buckwheat flour, à la Molly Wizenberg (waffle expert, writer, restaurateur).

**Makes about 8 waffles**

½ cup (120ml) warm water

1 (¼-ounce/7g) envelope active dry yeast

2 cups (475ml) milk, warmed

½ cup (115g) butter, melted

1 teaspoon salt

1 teaspoon sugar

2 cups (250g) all-purpose flour

2 large eggs

¼ teaspoon baking soda

1 Use a rather large mixing bowl—the batter will rise to double its original volume. Put the water in the mixing bowl and sprinkle in the yeast. Let stand to dissolve for 5 minutes.

2 Add the milk, butter, salt, sugar, and flour to the yeast mixture and beat until smooth and blended (Cunningham often used a hand rotary beater to get rid of the lumps). Cover the bowl with plastic wrap and let stand overnight at room temperature.

3 Just before cooking the waffles, beat in the eggs, add the baking soda, and stir until well mixed. The batter will be very thin. Pour about ½ to ¾ cup (120 to 180ml) of batter into a very hot waffle iron. Bake the waffles until they are golden and crisp. This batter will keep well for several days in the refrigerator.

# Snacks & Drinks

# Bar Nuts

FROM UNION SQUARE CAFÉ

Our memories of the entire bar nut genre are tinged with regret. The nuts are deeply salted to keep us reaching for our drinks; we are left parched and drunk.

But Danny Meyer's restaurants are more civilized than that. Union Square Café's bar nuts are legendary—as a dish, not a cocktail enabler. Only after you bake them naked—not caked in sugar, spice, or salt—do you toss them in what is essentially a five-ingredient dressing. It's a modest and just-damp mix, so the nuts hold onto their crunch, wearing only as much spicy butter as will cling to them. This means you can toast the nuts thoroughly, without worrying about burning the coating. You can also make the dressing (and drink half a beer) while the nuts toast, making this a multitasking, last-minute, classy party snack recipe that takes all of 10 minutes.

**Makes about 5 cups (800g)**

¼ pound (115g) each peeled peanuts, cashews, Brazil nuts, hazelnuts, walnuts, pecans, and whole unpeeled almonds, or 1¾ pounds (800g) unsalted assorted nuts

2 tablespoons coarsely chopped fresh rosemary

½ teaspoon cayenne pepper

2 teaspoons dark brown sugar

2 teaspoons kosher salt

1 tablespoon butter, melted

1 Preheat the oven to 350°F (175°C).

2 Toss the nuts in a large bowl to combine and spread them out on a cookie sheet. Toast in the oven until they become light golden brown, about 10 minutes.

3 In a large bowl, combine the rosemary, cayenne, brown sugar, salt, and melted butter. Thoroughly toss the warm toasted nuts with the spiced butter, adjust seasoning to taste, and serve warm.

# Deviled Eggs

FROM VIRGINIA WILLIS

Given our all-but-universal love for eggs, the deviled sort is strangely polarizing. The haters (like me, before I found this recipe) aren't about to pick one up at a party, because we know there's no turning back—no "just a taste," no hiding a tooth-marked egg in shame.

But it's never too late to change your mind: These are the devils that got me. Thanks to Virginia Willis, a French-trained chef with strong Southern roots, there's a whole lot of care and technique in this recipe, starting with the eggs being perfectly cooked. Technically, the eggs aren't hard-boiled, but rather hard-cooked (that is, left alone for 12 minutes in just-boiled water). The goal is to cook the yolks just enough to be firm—chalky, green-tinged yolks will only live on in our sad lunchroom memories. Willis's method results in yolks that are good and yellow, fluffed up with just enough condiments to go silken and loose. There is no overdosing on sweet, vinegary mayonnaise, no chunky pickle relish to mar the texture.

There is a secret ingredient, however: butter. Just a tad. It rounds and smooths over the more acidic ingredients, turns the filling creamy without overtaking it, and, as Willis says, "renders people unable to use the sense God gave a cat to stop eating."

## Makes 24

12 large eggs (at least a week old, if possible, for easier peeling)

⅓ cup (75g) mayonnaise

2 tablespoons unsalted butter, at room temperature

1 tablespoon Dijon mustard

Pinch of cayenne pepper

Coarse salt and freshly ground white pepper

2 tablespoons finely chopped fresh tarragon, chives, or chervil, plus leaves for garnish

1 To hard-cook the eggs, place them in a saucepan and add water to cover by 1 inch (2.5cm). Bring just up to a boil over high heat (you will see bubbles around the sides of the pot). Remove from the heat, cover, and let stand for 12 minutes. Drain the eggs and rinse them under cold running water. Set aside to cool completely.

2 To peel the cooked and cooled eggs, remove the shells by tapping each egg gently on the counter or sink all over to crackle it. Roll an egg between your hands to loosen the shell. Peel, starting at the large end, while holding the egg under cold running water; this facilitates peeling and also removes any stray shell fragments.

3 To prepare the filling, halve the peeled eggs lengthwise. Carefully remove the yolks. Set the whites aside. Pass the yolks through a fine-mesh strainer into a bowl, or place them in a food processor fitted with the metal blade. Blend the yolks, mayonnaise, butter, mustard, and cayenne, and mix until smooth; season with salt and white pepper. Add the finely chopped tarragon.

4 Spoon the mixture into a piping bag fitted with a large star tip or a medium sealable plastic bag with one of the corner tips snipped off. When you are ready to serve, pipe the yolk mixture into the whites. Garnish with additional herbs and serve immediately.

TO MAKE AHEAD: Unpeeled hard-cooked eggs can be refrigerated for up to 1 week. Or prepare the eggs, but don't assemble, up to 8 hours in advance of serving; refrigerate the whites covered with a damp towel in an airtight plastic container. Store the egg yolk mixture in the piping bag with the tip also covered with a damp paper towel. Knead the yolk mixture slightly to soften before filling the whites. The eggs may also be assembled and stored covered in the refrigerator for up to 2 hours. Any longer and the yolk mixture starts to form a crust.

# Basic Hummus

## FROM YOTAM OTTOLENGHI & SAMI TAMIMI

Most from-scratch hummus recipes call for simmering dried, soaked chickpeas for 1½ to 2 hours. Some even ask you to peel each chickpea for optimum smoothness. Yotam Ottolenghi and Sami Tamimi, cookbook authors and the team behind the Ottolenghi restaurants in London, cook theirs in 20 to 40 minutes. And no peeling. How, you ask?

The answer is baking soda, but not in the way you might think. Plenty of hummus recipes call for soaking or simmering the chickpeas with a little baking soda shaken into the water. It's all about pH: Alkaline environments soften legumes more quickly by weakening bonds between pectin molecules, while acidic environments keep them stubborn and stiff. This is why you never want to simmer beans with vinegar.

Ottolenghi and Tamimi go one step further in their recipe: After soaking, they sauté the drained chickpeas with baking soda for a few minutes before dumping in the water to simmer—a technique learned from Tamimi's grandmother. "We chose Sami's grandmother's way because we believe the friction helps the breaking down of the skins and gets the baking soda to penetrate the skin better," Ottolenghi told me. This brief, direct contact allows them to cook much faster and puree smoother. Without peeling.

A couple of final clever tricks seal the deal: You'll loosen the hummus with ice water at the end to cool it down quickly, keeping the flavors sharp. And then you'll rest it for 30 minutes, to let the flavors and textures settle in. And then you'll pour olive oil over it and scoop it up with torn bread in heavy, spilt-over measures.

### Serves 6

1¼ cups (250g) dried chickpeas
1 teaspoon baking soda
6½ cups (1.5L) water
1 cup plus 2 tablespoons (270g) tahini (light roast)
¼ cup (60ml) fresh lemon juice
4 cloves garlic, crushed
6½ tablespoons (100ml) ice cold water
Salt
Good-quality olive oil, to serve (optional)

1 Put the chickpeas in a large bowl and cover them with cold water at least twice their volume. Leave to soak overnight.

2 The next day, drain the chickpeas. Place a saucepan over high heat and add the drained chickpeas and baking soda. Cook for about 3 minutes, stirring constantly. Add the water and bring to a boil. Cook, skimming off any foam and any skins that float to the surface. The chickpeas will need to cook for 20 to 40 minutes, and sometimes even longer, depending on the type and freshness. Once done, they should be very tender, breaking up easily when pressed between your thumb and finger, almost but not quite mushy.

3 Drain the chickpeas. You should have roughly 3⅔ cups (600g) now. Place the chickpeas in a food processor and process until you get a stiff paste. Then, with the machine still running, add the tahini paste, lemon juice, garlic, and 1½ teaspoons of salt. Finally, slowly drizzle in the ice water and allow it to mix for about 5 minutes, until you get a very smooth and creamy paste.

4 Transfer the hummus to a bowl, cover the surface with plastic wrap, and let it rest for at least 30 minutes. Use straightaway or refrigerate until needed, taking it out of the fridge at least 30 minutes before serving. To serve, top with a layer of good-quality olive oil. This hummus will keep in the refrigerator for up to 3 days.

## One-Ingredient Whole Grain Crackers

ADAPTED FROM DAN BARBER

To make the simplest version of a whole grain cracker at his restaurant, Blue Hill at Stone Barns just outside New York City, Dan Barber purees boiled whole grains like freekeh or farro, spreads the loose pulp on a rimmed baking sheet about ⅛ inch (3mm) thick, and bakes it low until dry and crackly (say 300°F/150°C for about 2 hours). Doing this at home is just as straightforward. A cup of dried grains, boiled in abundant water till tender, then drained and pureed with a little of their cooking water, will make about 1 cookie sheet of crackers that handsomely show off the textures and flavors of whole grains. Once the sheet cools a bit, the crackers can be snapped off in irregular pieces. Salt is optional. The crackers pair nicely with hummus or herb jam (as pictured on page 47).

# No-Knead Bread

## FROM JIM LAHEY

The internet got its first viral recipe in 2006, when Mark Bittman brought Jim Lahey's technique for no-knead bread to light in the *New York Times*. Not-kneading tore through the blogosphere and, unlike the Bacon Explosion (the internet's second viral recipe), it stuck. Its instant and lasting popularity is not because kneading is so strenuous, but because it requires an understanding. You must form a relationship with your dough and sense when it's feeling too dry, or leathery, or loose (and how to fix it). These are worthy and satisfying pursuits, but they give cooks enough pause that bread baking once seemed reserved for dedicated hobbyists.

Then Bittman urged, "Let time do the work," and we listened. And we baked, and we blogged. And he wasn't kidding—after mixing the ingredients, you go on about your life until it's time to bake 12 or so hours later, flopping the dough around a couple times toward the end, then (carefully) flopping it once more into a preheated heavy pot or Dutch oven, which acts like a professional baker's steam-injected oven in miniature.

The loaf will taste (and look) better than most bread you can buy, with a dewy, wide-mawed crumb and dark crust that snaps under the knife. No doubt, you'll tell your friends—maybe even blog about it.

**Makes one 10-inch (25cm) round loaf (1¼ pounds/570g)**

3 cups (400g) bread flour
1¼ teaspoons (8g) table salt or fine sea salt
¼ teaspoon (1g) instant or other active dry yeast
1½ cups (360g) cool (55°F to 65°F/13°C to 18°C) water
Wheat bran, cornmeal, or additional flour for dusting

1 In a medium bowl, stir together the flour, salt, and yeast. Add the water and, using a wooden spoon or your hand, mix until you have a wet, sticky dough, about 30 seconds. Cover the bowl with a plate, kitchen towel, or plastic wrap, and let sit at room temperature (about 72°F/22°C), out of direct sunlight, until the surface is dotted with bubbles and the dough is doubled in size. This will take a minimum of 12 hours and (Lahey's preference) up to 18 hours. The slow rise—fermentation—is the key to flavor.

2 When the first fermentation is complete, generously dust a work surface (a wooden or plastic cutting board is fine) with flour. When you begin to pull the dough away from the bowl, it will cling in long, thin strands (this is the developed gluten), and it will be quite loose and sticky—do not add more flour. Use lightly floured hands or a bowl scraper or spatula to lift the edges of the dough in toward the center. Nudge and tuck the edges of the dough to make it round.

3 Place a cotton or linen kitchen towel or a large cloth napkin on your work surface and generously dust the cloth with wheat bran, cornmeal, or flour. Use your hands or a bowl scraper or wooden spatula to gently lift the dough onto the towel, so it is seam side down. If the dough is tacky, dust the top lightly with wheat bran, cornmeal, or flour. Fold the ends of the towel loosely over the dough to cover it and place it in a

CONTINUED

# No-Knead Bread

## Continued

warm, draft-free spot to rise for 1 to 2 hours. The dough is ready when it is almost doubled. If you gently poke it with your finger, making an indentation about ¼ inch (6mm) deep, it should hold the impression. If it doesn't, let it rise for another 15 minutes.

4 Half an hour before the end of the second rise, preheat the oven to 475°F (245°C) with a rack in the lower third position, and place a covered 4½- to 5½-quart (4.5 to 5L) heavy pot in the center of the rack.

5 Using pot holders, carefully remove the preheated pot from the oven and uncover it. Unfold the kitchen towel, lift up the dough—either on the towel or in your hand—and quickly but gently invert it into the pot so the dough lands seam side up. Cover the pot and bake for 30 minutes.

6 Remove the lid and continue baking until the bread is a deep chestnut color but not burnt, 15 to 30 minutes more. Use a heatproof spatula or pot holders to carefully lift the bread out of the pot and place it on a rack to cool thoroughly. Don't slice or tear into it until it has cooled, which usually takes at least an hour.

# Grilled Favas

## FROM IGNACIO MATTOS

If you're shelling fava beans for more than just yourself—cracking open each chubby pod, peeling away every bean's little green wetsuit, and leaving a massive pile of detritus in your wake—you either love the people you're cooking for with unshakeable devotion or you are a restaurant prep cook. Hannibal Lecter—infamous lover of favas—preferred to dine alone.

But favas don't deserve their high-maintenance reputation. The fact is they were born edible, from pod to peel to bean. As with chard stems (page 183) or unripe peaches (page 77), you just have to know what to do with them. To eat the whole fava (and not waste a thing), do as chef Ignacio Mattos does and throw them on the grill. Smoke and char do great things for favas' thick-walled pods and skins, and they'll soften enough that you can eat them with your hands. (If you don't have a grill, a hot cast-iron skillet or broiler works, too.)

It helps to seek out the smallest, cutest favas. But even if you're stuck with the big, gnarly ones, you can eat the pods you want, and just pop out the inner beans for the ones you don't—they'll still slide out more easily after they've been cooked.

You'll toss them in a feisty marinade—a bit fuses on as they sear on the grill. Then you'll put them right back in the pool of marinade to latch onto the flavors anew. Then you will hit them with lemon and what seems like a crazy amount of anchovy. But trust Mattos: I tasted one pod before adding any and was ready to cast them aside. Then I stirred in the whole tin's worth of anchovy and ate the rest of the bowl without sitting down. So, in this way, these are still favas for one. But now at least they're scalable.

### Serves 4 to 6

1 pound (450g) fresh fava beans in their pods, the younger the better

1 teaspoon fleur de sel, plus more as needed

1 teaspoon ground chile

1 teaspoon picked rosemary leaves

3 to 4 cloves garlic, chopped

¼ cup (60ml) extra-virgin olive oil, plus more to finish

2 tablespoons water

1 lemon

7 to 8 anchovies canned in oil, finely chopped

Handful of toasted bread crumbs (optional)

1 Prepare a medium-hot fire in a gas or charcoal grill.

2 Mix together the fava beans, fleur de sel, ground chile, rosemary, garlic, olive oil, and water in a large bowl. Toss to coat the fava pods, then place them on the grill over medium-high heat. Grill the favas for several minutes, until charred, then flip them over and char the other side, cooking until the pods seem about to open.

3 Remove the pods from the grill, return them to the mixing bowl, and squeeze the lemon over them. Toss the pods to coat. Add the anchovies to the bowl, mixing well. Check the seasoning, and add salt, if necessary.

4 Place the pods on a serving platter, drizzle to taste with olive oil, and sprinkle the bread crumbs on top. Serve hot or at room temperature; eat with your hands.

# Classic Guacamole

## FROM ROBERTO SANTIBAÑEZ

What Mexican chef and cookbook author Roberto Santibañez wants cooks to realize is this: "There is a very important textural thing to guacamole—we never really mush up the avocado. You want to feel everything."

In his recipe, the ingredients are what you'd expect, but by handling them differently, your standard for great guacamole will shift. You won't want to leave chunky bits of onion and chile to stumble on anymore. Nor will you want to grind the avocado into a creamy, homogenous mass. Instead, with a mortar and pestle, the side of a big knife, or even a fork, Santibañez pulverizes chile, onion, cilantro, and salt into a bright green slurry, then gently folds in cubed avocado. He crushes only enough of the avocado to warrant its consideration as a dip rather than a salad, but leaves the rest of the cubes intact—as he says, "a bit like salad properly dressed in vinaigrette."

More chopped cilantro and (optional) lime juice finish it off, and you have a dip that ignites as it first hits your tongue, then cools as you break through each lump of clean, creamy avocado.

**Makes about 1¾ cups (415ml)**

2 tablespoons finely chopped white onion

1 tablespoon minced fresh serrano or jalapeño chile, including seeds, plus more to taste

½ teaspoon kosher salt, or ¼ teaspoon fine salt

¼ cup (5g) chopped cilantro, divided

1 large or 2 small ripe Mexican Hass avocados, halved and pitted

A squeeze of lime, if desired

1 Mash the onion, chile, salt (the coarseness of kosher salt helps you make the paste), and half of the cilantro to a paste in a *molcajete* or other mortar. You can also mince and mash the ingredients together on a cutting board with a large knife or a fork, and then transfer the paste to a bowl.

2 Score the flesh in the avocado halves in a crosshatch pattern (not through the skin) with a knife and then scoop it with a spoon into the mortar or bowl. Toss well, then add the rest of the cilantro and mash coarsely with a pestle or a fork. Season to taste with lime juice and additional chile and salt. Serve immediately.

# Herb Jam with Olives & Lemon

## FROM PAULA WOLFERT

Bundles of herbs are too often the victims of crisper drawer abandonment. One solution is to store them like a bouquet of flowers: upright in a jar in the fridge, stems dangling in fresh water, and tops protected by a plastic bag secured by a rubber band around the base. If you remember to change the water every few days, your herbs will last for an unnervingly long time.

I usually don't remember to do this. And even when I do, those herbs can't defy their fate forever. And they don't have to: Put them into a traditional Moroccan green spread, translated for the average home cook's kitchen by Paula Wolfert—expert on Mediterranean cooking and author of eight books on the subject.

It doesn't matter if your herbs are starting to lose their edge because you're about to cook the daylights out of them. You'll steam your orphaned herbs and greens, then chop, sauté, and mash them into a jam with some heady spices and pantry staples. The result is surprisingly meaty for something with so much green in it.

Sure, this jam isn't here to win beauty pageants—it's glorified mulch, really. If this concerns you, tuck it into a sandwich or omelet, or stir some into a soup as you would pistou. Or just serve it on a handsome plate with rustic one-ingredient crackers (page 37).

### GENIUS TIP

Wolfert calls for baby spinach and a specific cocktail of parsley, cilantro, and celery leaves, but you can substitute whatever greens and herbs need using up.

**Serves 6 (makes about 1½ cups/360ml)**

4 large cloves garlic, halved

1 pound (450g) baby spinach leaves

1 large bunch flat-leaf parsley, stems discarded

½ cup (10g) celery leaves, coarsely chopped

½ cup (10g) cilantro leaves, stems discarded

¼ cup (60ml) extra-virgin olive oil, plus more as needed

12 oil-cured black olives, pitted, rinsed, and coarsely chopped

1¼ teaspoons Spanish sweet smoked paprika (pimentón de la Vera)

Pinch of cayenne pepper

Pinch of ground cumin

1 tablespoon fresh lemon juice, or more to taste

Salt and freshly ground black pepper

1 Put the garlic cloves in a large steamer basket set over a pan of simmering water and top with the spinach, parsley, celery, and cilantro. Cover and steam until the garlic is soft and the greens are very tender, about 15 minutes. Let cool, then squeeze the greens dry, finely chop, and set aside. Using the back of a fork, mash the garlic cloves.

2 In a medium *cazuela* set over a flame-tamer, or in a heavy-bottomed skillet, heat 1 tablespoon of the olive oil until shimmering. Add the mashed garlic, olives, paprika, cayenne, and cumin and stir over medium-high heat for 30 seconds, or until fragrant. Add the greens and cook, mashing and stirring, until soft and dry and somewhat smooth, about 15 minutes.

3 Remove from the heat and let cool to room temperature. Mash in the remaining 3 tablespoons olive oil. Refrigerate, tightly sealed, for at least 1 day and up to 4 days.

4 To serve, return to room temperature. Stir in the lemon juice and, if it seems too thick, thin to a spreadable consistency with water or olive oil. Season with salt and pepper.

# Salt-Crusted Potatoes with Cilantro Mojo

FROM JOSÉ PIZARRO

This appetizer from José Pizarro, Spanish cookbook author and restaurateur, will kick off a party with heart-thumping flavors, invite ice-breaking questions (are those fossils? how do I eat them?), and break down any notions of proper etiquette (spoiler: Everyone's fingers are going to get salty).

You're essentially just boiling potatoes. But you do it in a wide, shallow pan, in a single layer, without a lid. And with a lot of sea salt. The water bubbles away, and in 20 minutes, the potatoes have sort of steam-boiled tender. A dusty layer of salt covers the potatoes like ash. The outsides look fiercely salty, but the middles are creamy and gently seasoned, so an initial slap of salt and pop of taut skin quickly gives way to buttery flesh. The kicker is a cuminy, garlicky cilantro mojo—a green sauce you bang out in a mortar and pestle or mini food processor, perfect for dragging your crusty potatoes across.

Altogether it's so good you won't want to wait for your next dinner party to make it again. And that's okay—it makes a great any-night side, too. Just grill a steak or chop or butterflied chicken to go with it, and the mojo will get even more play.

### GENIUS TIP

This is a forgiving technique—it works in a variety of pans, with various kinds of salt, and always comes out perfectly. The salt dissolves in the water, which then evaporates to form the crust—you end up leaving a lot of salt behind in the pan, so any difference in saltiness is somewhat negligible.

Serves 6

### SALT-CRUSTED POTATOES

2¼ pounds (1kg) evenly sized waxy new potatoes, such as fingerling, scrubbed but unpeeled

2 tablespoons sea salt flakes

### CILANTRO MOJO

3 large cloves garlic, roughly chopped

1 green chile, seeded and chopped

1 teaspoon sea salt flakes

Leaves from a bunch of fresh cilantro, roughly chopped

1 teaspoon freshly ground cumin seeds

Scant ½ cup (120ml) extra-virgin olive oil

2 teaspoons white wine vinegar, muscatel if possible

1 **To make the potatoes,** put the potatoes in a wide, shallow pan in which they fit in a single layer. Add 2 tablespoons of salt and 1 quart (1L) of cold water (just enough to cover), bring to a boil, and leave to boil rapidly until the water has evaporated. Test one of the larger potatoes for tenderness with the tip of a paring knife. If there's still some resistance, add more water and continue boiling. Once the potatoes are tender and the water has evaporated, turn the heat to low and continue to cook for a few minutes, gently turning the potatoes over occasionally, until they are dry and the skins are wrinkled and covered in a thin crust of salt.

2 **Meanwhile, make the cilantro mojo.** Put the garlic, chile, and salt in a mortar and pound into a paste. Add the cilantro and pound until the leaves are incorporated into the paste. Add the cumin and gradually mix in the oil to make a smooth sauce. Just before serving, stir in the vinegar and spoon into a small bowl.

3 Pile the hot potatoes onto a plate and serve with the mojo, instructing your guests to rub off as much salt from the potatoes as they wish before dipping them in the sauce.

# Watermelon, Mint & Cider Vinegar Tonic

## FROM LOUISA SHAFIA

While there's only so much lemonade you can drink in the hot sun before the sugar starts to go to your head—and boozy drinks pose a similar, sloppier problem—this is an elixir you could drink all day.

Even if drinking vinegar sounds like a dare, it's age-old in lots of places, a means of preserving fruit in pickled, drinkable form as much as a way to cool off.

Louisa Shafia, author of *The New Persian Kitchen*, takes the traditional Iranian version called *sekanjabin*—which is often made with white vinegar and sugar—and puts her own modern stamp on it, steeping watermelon in cider vinegar, honey, and mint. A bonus: After straining to get your drink concentrate, you get to eat the pickled watermelon (a mild-tempered fruit gets a lot more interesting once it takes up a little minty brine).

And because it's a grown-up drink without alcohol, you can take the tonic on a picnic, at any park, without having to look side-eyed at cops that might pass by. You can stare them straight in the face and tell them what you're drinking: vinegar.

### GENIUS TIPS

Shafia suggests adding a few slices of ginger, fresh rose petals, or a stalk of crushed lemongrass or, instead of watermelon, swapping in cherries (sweet or sour), sliced apricots, peaches, plums, or grapes.

**Makes 5 cups (1.2L) concentrate, enough for twenty 1-cup (240g) servings of tonic**

3 cups (710ml) water, plus more to serve

¼ teaspoon fine sea salt

1 cup (340g) good-quality honey

6 cups (910g) coarsely chopped watermelon

1 cup (25g) tightly packed fresh spearmint

1 cup (240ml) cider vinegar

Ice cubes

Chopped watermelon, sliced unwaxed cucumber, and spearmint, for garnish

1 Bring the water and the salt to a boil in a saucepan. Add the honey, stir to dissolve, and remove from the heat.

2 Combine the watermelon and mint in a large bowl. Stir in the honey water and let cool to room temperature, then add the vinegar. Steep the mixture in the refrigerator for several hours or up to overnight.

3 Strain the mixture and eat the watermelon chunks, if desired. Pour the concentrate into a clean glass jar, and store in the refrigerator for up to 1 week.

4 To serve, pour ¼ cup (60ml) of the concentrate into a glass over ice and dilute with ¾ cup (180ml) of water. Garnish with watermelon, cucumber, and mint.

# Tomato Water Bloody Mary

## FROM TODD THRASHER

We're in luck: As soon as it gets too hot to really want a drink thick with tomato puree and horseradish, the real tomatoes come in—and we can have an even better Bloody Mary. Restaurant Eve's general manager, sommelier, and liquid savant, Todd Thrasher, who's known for working in-season produce into his cocktails, makes them with tomato water instead.

The liquid that leaches from a tomato is deceptively colorless, but it tastes like ripe, raw summer distilled into a cup. Add lemongrass, red onion, and serrano and you have borderline tomato consommé, with none of the fuss and technique.

Making infused tomato water the night before sounds (and perhaps, in its paleness, looks) fussy, but the method is surprisingly straightforward and loose. You pile a bunch of fresh summer ingredients into a food processor, make something resembling gazpacho, then pour it into a cloth-lined strainer to settle overnight. When it's time for brunch, you add lemon, lime, and orange juices and citron (or, in desperation, regular) vodka. Served tall, it's almost dangerously quenching for the dog days, and the vodka, tomato, spice, and citrus play the Bloody Mary card well, without reminding anyone of cocktail sauce.

### GENIUS TIPS

Michael Ruhlman uses tomato water to sauce pastas in the summer (simmered briefly with garlic and thickened only with a little butter).

You can also use it to brighten soups, salad dressings, and juices.

**Makes 4 drinks**

TOMATO WATER

4 large beefsteak tomatoes, quartered

½ serrano chile, coarsely chopped

¼ red onion, coarsely chopped

One 3-inch (7.5cm) piece of lemongrass, tough outer leaves removed and coarsely chopped

Small pinch of sugar

Large pinch of salt

½ lime

½ lemon

½ orange

COCKTAIL

Ice

2 cups (475ml) tomato water

6 ounces (¾ cup/180ml) Grey Goose Le Citron (or any citrus vodka)

4 cherry tomatoes, for garnish

1 **To make the tomato water,** puree the tomatoes, chile, onion, lemongrass, sugar, and salt in a food processor, until smooth. Line a large strainer with a double layer of cheesecloth, and set the strainer over a nonreactive bowl. Pour the puree into the strainer and refrigerate overnight.

2 Gather the sides of the cheesecloth up over the puree to form a large sack and squeeze gently to extract the last bits of water. Discard the cheesecloth and its contents. Set a strainer over the bowl and squeeze in the lime, lemon, and orange juices. Stir well.

3 **To make the cocktails,** fill four highball glasses with ice. In each, combine 4 ounces (½ cup/120ml) tomato water and 1½ ounces (3 tablespoons/45ml) vodka and stir. Garnish with cherry tomatoes.

# Spiced Red Wine (Ypocras)

## FROM ANNE WILLAN

Wouldn't it be nice if we could bottle the cozy mulled wine of holiday parties and snowy ski weekends to sip whenever we want? And maybe not cook all the booze away?

We can. In fact, we've been doing it since the 1300s. I'm talking about a spiced red wine called *ypocras,* unearthed from medieval times and modernized by Anne Willan, food historian, cookbook author, and founder of La Varenne cooking school.

Like sangria, *ypocras* is never cooked—it's simply infused with spices and sugar at room temperature, so the booze doesn't fizzle away. As Willan explains, this method "was a way of preserving wine before bottles and corks," and the spiced wine will keep for a month. It also happens to be lovely for sipping: sweet and winey like port, with four heady spices breathing in the fire of a harder aperitif.

It's a simple potion to make—mix spices with brown sugar and wine, wait a day or two, strain. If you can find mace and grains of paradise (available at specialty grocers or online), you will be authentically medieval. If not, you can substitute an equal amount of nutmeg and black pepper, respectively.

Bookmark this recipe for the holidays. It's also good to keep around—to sip after dinner, or before, or with steak, cheese, or cookies, or when you're in the bathtub. Just like they did in the 1300s.

### GENIUS TIPS

You can also cook with *ypocras* and mix it into cocktails. Willan uses it to marinate and braise salmon, poach whole pears and peaches (diluted with an equal amount of water), and top off glasses of sparkling white wine.

**Makes about 3 cups (750ml)**

1 cup (200g) lightly packed brown sugar

1 tablespoon ground cinnamon

1 tablespoon ground mace (or substitute an equal amount of grated nutmeg)

1½ teaspoons ground cloves

1½ teaspoons ground grains of paradise (or substitute an equal amount of freshly ground black pepper)

1 bottle (750ml) fruity red wine, such as Merlot

1 In a nonreactive bowl, stir together the brown sugar, cinnamon, mace, cloves, and grains of paradise. Add the wine and stir well. Leave for 10 minutes, then stir again to dissolve the sugar fully. Cover tightly and leave at room temperature for 1 to 2 days.

2 Strain the wine mixture through a strainer lined with a double layer of cheesecloth into a bowl. A brown deposit will be left on the cheesecloth. Rinse it off and strain the wine at least once more through the cheesecloth to clarify it as well as possible. Store the wine in an airtight container (if you like, use the original bottle) at room temperature. It will keep for up to 1 month.

NOTE: If you'd like to grind your own spices, allow ¼ ounce (7g) per tablespoon.

# Cliff Old Fashioned

FROM DAVE ARNOLD

There's little you'd want to do to an old fashioned: It's the original cocktail, made from the simplest ingredients you can find in a home bar—whiskey, sugar, bitters—stirred in a glass with an ice cube, topped with an orange twist, and sipped. Some would say you oughtn't mess with it at all.

But that hasn't stopped us from contorting it with absinthe or tequila, adding funky liqueurs or muddled fruit. That's fine, if you're inclined to tinker and have a well-stocked liquor cabinet. But there's a subtler way to tweak the classic that only asks that you visit your spice drawer, find the coriander and crushed red pepper flakes, and add them into a simple syrup for a little extra flowery sting.

The effect is light-handed, which doesn't come as a surprise from Dave Arnold and the rest of the precise, culinary-minded team at Booker & Dax. But where their M.O. is generally about high technology and flair—cask-aged liqueurs, cocktails carbonated in the bottle, centrifuges, and dry ice—anyone who has a bottle of whiskey can make this at home.

**Makes 1 cocktail**

### CORIANDER SYRUP

Scant ½ cup (120ml) water

Scant ½ cup (100g) sugar

1 tablespoon coriander seeds

1½ teaspoons crushed red pepper flakes

### COCKTAIL

2 ounces (¼ cup/60ml) whiskey, preferably Yamazaki 12-year single malt or Rittenhouse 100-proof rye

Scant ½ ounce (1 tablespoon/15ml) coriander syrup

2 dashes Angostura bitters

Orange twist

1 **To make the coriander syrup,** combine the water, sugar, coriander seeds, and ½ teaspoon of the crushed red pepper in a saucepan. Bring to a boil, turn off the heat, then add the remaining teaspoon of crushed red pepper. Stir and let steep, tasting occasionally, until the flavor of the spices in the syrup hits the back of your throat but does not overwhelm the mixture. Strain through a double layer of cheesecloth or a fine-mesh chinois, then let cool before using. Stored tightly sealed in the refrigerator, the syrup will keep for 1 week. Makes about ½ cup (120ml).

2 **To make the cocktail,** combine all the ingredients except the orange twist in an old fashioned glass. Add one large chunk of ice and stir until chilled. Twist a large piece of orange zest over the drink and drop into the glass.

# Soups & Salads

# Romaine Hearts with Caesar Salad Dressing

## FROM FRANKIES SPUNTINO

This Caesar dressing breaks most every rule of the classic recipe and dispenses with several key ingredients, and yet, after taking a bite, you'll identify it immediately.

It borrows the things we love most about Caesar: the anchovy, the garlic, the Worcestershire, and the bright acidity—although here instead of lemon it comes from red wine vinegar and Tabasco. Pecorino—whose funkiness fits in well here—takes the place of Parmesan. The egg and oil are replaced with jarred Hellmann's, or Best Foods, mayo. Nothing about this seems like a good idea.

It's appropriate that this heretical and fiercely convenient recipe comes from Frank Falcinelli and Frank Castronuovo—known colloquially as the Franks—founders of a small New York restaurant empire built on neoclassical Italian-American comfort food.

You make the dressing in the blender (no mincing, no whisking) and there is no egg, so you can keep it in the fridge all week, using it on any salad and any random crudité-like snack, on roasted vegetables and sandwiches and pizza. You can take it to work for lunch, or serve it at picnics and barbecues without worry. But, most importantly, these are all things you will *want* to do, because the dressing—incorrect as it may be—is awfully good.

### Serves 4 to 6

3 hearts of romaine (pull away the floppiest, greenest outer leaves)

⅓ cup (35g) grated Pecorino Romano, plus additional for serving

½ cup (110g) Hellmann's mayonnaise

¼ cup (60ml) water, plus more as needed

1½ teaspoons red wine vinegar

1 clove garlic

2 anchovy fillets

¼ teaspoon Worcestershire sauce

¼ teaspoon Tabasco sauce

8 turns freshly ground white pepper

Fine sea salt, if needed

Freshly ground black pepper

1 Trim the root ends from the romaine, separate the leaves, and wash and dry them. Put the lettuce in the fridge to chill while you prepare the dressing.

2 Combine ¼ cup (25g) of the Pecorino with the remaining ingredients (except the black pepper) in a blender and puree until the dressing is smooth. (If you don't have a blender, mince the garlic and anchovy, and whisk them together with the rest of the dressing ingredients.) Taste and add salt if necessary; the cheese, Hellmann's, Worcestershire, and anchovies are all salty, so you probably won't need any additional salt. Loosen the dressing with more water as needed.

3 Toss the chilled lettuce with the dressing in a large bowl. Transfer to serving plates or a serving platter and finish with a generous crowning of the remaining grated cheese and a few turns of black pepper. Serve at once.

# Fresh Fig & Mint Salad

FROM RICHARD OLNEY

The genius of this attention-grabbing recipe lies in French cooking master Richard Olney's bizarre but clever selection of ingredients, and the ways he harnessed their best traits.

First, you muddle fresh mint in lemon juice and let it steep for 30 minutes. Then you strain out the battered leaves, while their cooling oils remain. Next, you stir in some salt, then some cream (Olney liked his thick and unpasteurized). The acid in the lemon juice thickens the cream effortlessly, without curdling it. (It does this so well that if you use a whisk and not a spoon, you may unintentionally end up with tart whipped cream—which isn't a bad thing, but Olney was going for something closer to half-whipped.) As dressings go, this isn't like any we know—instead, it's akin to a sharper, fresher, instant crème fraîche or yogurt.

But it gets odder still: You'll have chilled the figs in the coldest part of the fridge before scattering them on the plate with cream, prosciutto, and more mint. So many foods taste better at room temperature, their flavors looser and more developed. But here, the coolness means that a plate that could feel heavy—with the salty fat of prosciutto, the jammy richness of figs, and cream—doesn't.

### GENIUS TIPS

Feel free to go rogue on the presentation. If you don't want to bother crisscrossing the figs and opening them up like baked potatoes, just cut them in half, or slice them thickly. Same goes for the prosciutto: No patience for carving a soft pile into matchsticks? Tear it into ragged bites, or just lay down a slice and provide knives for your guests. You're the boss of this beautiful, alien salad. Make it your own.

**Serves 5 or 6**

2 pounds (900g) ripe figs, freshly picked if possible

3 thin slices prosciutto, fat removed

12 to 15 leaves fresh mint

Juice of 1 lemon

Salt

¼ cup (60ml) heavy cream

1 Peel the figs (or don't—I didn't) and cut a bit more than halfway down from the stem end, making two incisions in the form of a cross. Press gently from the sides to open them slightly (as one does with a baked potato). Arrange the figs closely on a serving dish and chill for about 1 hour in the coldest part of the refrigerator (not the freezer).

2 Cut the prosciutto into fine julienne strips about 1 inch (2.5cm) in length and matchstick width.

3 Crush about half of the mint leaves in the lemon juice and leave to macerate for 20 to 30 minutes, then discard the crushed leaves.

4 Dissolve the salt into the lemon juice and slowly stir in the cream—the acid of the lemon will thicken it somewhat, and its addition in small quantities at a time with continued stirring encourages the thickening. Taste and add salt, if necessary.

5 Plate as desired. Olney's recommendation: Sprinkle the figs with half of the sliced prosciutto, spoon over the cream sauce, distribute the remaining prosciutto on the surface, and decorate with the remaining mint leaves.

# "Use a Spoon" Chopped Salad

### FROM MICHEL NISCHAN

It's easy to stress sourcing ingredients at their peak and taking care not to over (or under) dress a salad, but how you eat it can be just as important. When Paul Newman opened The Dressing Room with chef Michel Nischan in Westport, Connecticut, he wanted a chopped salad on the menu, one where the ingredients would be cut so fine you could eat it with a spoon.

Instead of working with a standard palette of fresh ingredients, which could only get him so far, Nischan took a few of the more wishy-washy contenders and gave them a makeover. Carrots, celery, and bell pepper get quick pickled and come into brighter focus. A bonus: After they soak in vinegar for a spell, the vinegar inherits some of their character, too. Into the dressing it goes.

Every spoonful is jumbled with the snap of acid and tugs of bitter, sweet, and clean, with no shortage of toasted almond slivers and cold nubs of fresh goat cheese slipping in here and there to finish the dressing's work.

**Serves 6**

1½ cups (360ml) Riesling vinegar or other white wine vinegar

3 celery ribs, cut into ¼-inch (6mm) dice

2 carrots, peeled and cut into ¼-inch (6mm) dice

1 large red bell pepper, seeded and cut into ¼-inch (6mm) dice

1 heirloom apple, such as Cox's Orange Pippin or Roxbury Russet, peeled, cored, and cut into ¼-inch (6mm) dice

½ large cucumber, peeled, seeded, and cut into ¼-inch (6mm) dice

1 cup (40g) sliced radicchio

1 cup (40g) sliced arugula

1 cup (70g) thinly sliced napa, Savoy, or other soft cabbage

3 tablespoons extra-virgin olive oil

Sea salt and freshly ground black pepper

1½ cups (170g) crumbled soft local goat cheese

½ cup (55g) toasted almond slivers

1 Bring the vinegar to a simmer in a saucepan over medium heat. Add the celery and carrots. Remove the pan from the heat. Set aside to cool. When the vinegar is cool, add the bell pepper. Cover and refrigerate until cold. Strain the chilled vegetables through a sieve. Reserve the vinegar and vegetables separately.

2 Mix together the apple, cucumber, radicchio, arugula, cabbage, and the reserved vegetables in a large bowl. Add ¼ cup (60ml) of the reserved vinegar and the oil and toss well. Season to taste with salt and pepper. Add the goat cheese and almonds to the bowl and toss to mix. Divide among six bowls or plates and serve.

# Radicchio Salad with Manchego Vinaigrette

FROM TORO BRAVO

When we think about dressing up our everyday salads, we tend to think of what we can add. We build and layer, until our salad resembles leafy greens about as much as it does a 1970s variety hour. Here, instead, is salad made of one ingredient, plus dressing and cheese—from Toro Bravo, a tapas restaurant in Portland, Oregon. Austere as this salad may seem, it's got two tricks that will make you better at making all of your salads.

First up: Slivers of raw onion and spicy pricks of garlic seem like a good idea, until you're breathing fire 30 minutes later. Toro Bravo's answer: Infuse the vinegar with chopped red onion for an hour, then remove it. The vinegar is left richer and more complex, without the oppressive oniony kickback.

Once you add dressing to radicchio leaves or other slippery lettuces, it tends to bounce off into the bottom of the bowl. This is where the second trick comes in. You'll toss the dressed leaves again with a dusting of finely grated Manchego to help the coating stick. Everything you need is right here.

### Serves 4 to 8

2 to 3 heads radicchio
¼ cup (60ml) good-quality balsamic vinegar
¼ cup (60ml) good-quality sherry vinegar
1 red onion, chopped
1 tablespoon honey
¾ cup (180ml) olive oil
1½ cups (150g) finely grated Manchego cheese
Salt

1 Remove the cores from the radicchio and discard. Chop into 1-inch (2.5cm) pieces. You should have 4 quarts (3.8L). Pour 1 gallon of water into a large bowl and add enough ice to make the water icy cold. Once cold, strain out the ice and add the radicchio to the water. Let it sit for 15 minutes to remove some of its bitterness. Strain and then spin in a salad spinner until dry. Fluff the dried radicchio.

2 In a large bowl, combine the balsamic vinegar, sherry vinegar, and chopped red onion. Break the onion up into pieces so that all of that oniony flavor gets into the vinegar. (Note: If you want to quick pickle and eat the onions themselves, Food52 contributor hardlikearmour suggests adding the honey now, too.) Let it sit for 1 hour and then strain out the onions.

3 Add the honey and olive oil to the strained vinegars and whisk. Using your hands, toss the radicchio with the dressing until evenly coated. Add 1 cup (100g) of the Manchego, salt, and toss again.

4 To serve, top the salad in a bowl with the remaining ½ cup (50g) of grated Manchego or distribute the salad and cheese among four to eight bowls or plates.

## Garlic-Scented Tomato Salad
ADAPTED FROM MARCELLA HAZAN

Steeping alliums in vinegar is a good trick for improving any salad dressing, but here is one variation you shouldn't miss when tomatoes are in season. Of this stripped down salad, Marcella Hazan wrote on her Facebook page in 2012, "It has the potential to eclipse every other experience of tomatoes you may have had."

Peel and smash 4 to 5 garlic cloves and steep them with 1 to 2 teaspoons salt and 2 tablespoons of red wine vinegar in a bowl for at least 20 minutes. Slice 2 pounds (900g) of fresh, ripe round or plum tomatoes with a serrated knife—Hazan has you skin them first, but this isn't strictly necessary. Spread them in a deep serving platter and, just before serving, scatter with a dozen torn basil leaves. Holding back the garlic, pour the vinegar over the tomatoes and dress with good, fruity olive oil, then taste and correct, if necessary, for salt and vinegar. Serves 4 to 6.

# Warm Squash & Chickpea Salad with Tahini

## FROM MORO

Once we realize that salad doesn't have to mean lettuce, our options open up. This one, from Moro restaurant in London, starts with warm roasted squash tossed with chickpeas (best cooked from scratch, but a can will do). It's hefty enough to be the only thing on the table, light enough not to make you groggy, and lively enough to make winter squash a lot more compelling. It also happens to be vegan, but even a person who expects meat at every meal will be content with a bowl of this.

Vinaigrette might disappear into the squash and slide off the chickpeas. This is where tahini comes in: It's a vegan means of adding smoke, protein, creaminess, and substance (also an impressive carrier of garlic, lemon, and salt). With just the squash, chickpeas, and tahini, you might think your bowl will look like a burnt sienna paint strip—a good fistful of green cilantro leaves and some purple onion bits will take care of that.

---

**GENIUS TIP**

Maybe you want the grip of sweet raw red onion to shake up your mouth. Maybe you don't. If you'd prefer to tone it down, just soak the onion bits in cold water for 15 minutes or so after chopping, then drain well.

**Serves 4**

2 pounds (900g) winter squash, peeled, seeded, and cut into 1-inch (2.5cm) cubes (see photos, pages 72–73)

1 clove garlic, crushed

½ teaspoon ground allspice

2 tablespoons olive oil

Sea salt and black pepper

1½ cups (250g) home-cooked chickpeas or one (425g) can cooked chickpeas, drained

½ small red onion, finely chopped

¼ cup (5g) roughly chopped fresh cilantro

**TAHINI SAUCE**

1 clove garlic, crushed to a paste with a pinch of salt

3½ tablespoons fresh lemon juice

3 tablespoons tahini paste

2 tablespoons water, plus more if needed

2 tablespoons extra-virgin olive oil, plus more to taste

1 Preheat the oven to 425°F (220°C). Line a baking sheet with parchment paper.

2 Toss the squash with the garlic, allspice, olive oil, and some salt and pepper. Place on the baking sheet and roast for 20 to 25 minutes, or until soft. Allow to cool slightly.

3 **Meanwhile, make the tahini sauce.** Mix the crushed garlic with the lemon juice and add the tahini paste. Now thin with the water and olive oil, and check for seasoning. You should taste a balance between the nutty tahini and lemon.

4 To assemble the salad, place the squash, chickpeas, red onion, and cilantro in a mixing bowl. Pour on the tahini sauce and toss carefully. Season with salt and pepper and add more oil to taste. Serve immediately.

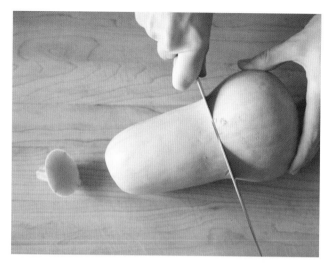

# Kale Salad

FROM NORTHERN SPY FOOD CO.

Raw kale is like any other green we've ever put to dressing—just a little more resilient. And that's a very helpful trait, making it an ideal leafy salad to make ahead for company or tomorrow's lunch.

This particular kale salad from Northern Spy restaurant in New York is at once substantial and spry. It's dressed with just lemon and olive oil, making it a bit like a raw version at a health store salad bar—but filled out with roasted kabocha squash, almonds, and two kinds of cheese. Depending on the season, Northern Spy trades out the kabocha for fresh apricots, kohlrabi, or pattypan squash. I sometimes go with slices of apple or persimmon. Kale's amenable.

And guess what? No massaging, unless you have to settle for a huskier bunch of curly kale. You can toss lacinato kale (also called Tuscan kale, cavolo nero, and dinosaur kale) without getting quite so handsy—leaving you with still-bouncy wisps of green, sweet pockets of squash, pops of almond, and all that cheese.

---

### GENIUS TIP

Another way to riff on kale salad: toasted bread crumbs. The thrill of stumbling on a crouton is spread across the entire salad, in more attainable bites. The effect isn't dissimilar to the craggy crust we love on fried food, except there's a bright salad under it all.

The cavolo nero salad at Franny's restaurant in Brooklyn is nothing more than kale dressed with smashed garlic, lemon juice, olive oil, crushed red pepper flakes, Pecorino, and bread crumbs toasted in butter. Do make your own fresh bread crumbs for this, by grinding up stale bread in a food processor or on a box grater. The bread crumbs will lose their crunch if you mix them in ahead, so either save them separately or plan on eating it all right away.

### Serves 2

½ cup (70g) peeled, cubed kabocha, butternut, or other winter squash

Extra-virgin olive oil

Salt and freshly ground black pepper

1 bunch kale (preferably lacinato or dinosaur kale), ribs removed and leaves finely sliced, about 2½ cups (170g)

¼ cup (35g) almonds, cut roughly in half

¼ cup (35g) crumbled or finely chopped Cabot Clothbound Cheddar (or any good, aged cheddar—if you can't find aged cheddar, use Parmesan)

Fresh lemon juice

Pecorino or other hard cheese, for shaving (optional)

1 Preheat the oven to 425°F (220°C). Line a baking sheet with parchment paper.

2 Toss the squash cubes in just enough oil to coat and season with salt and pepper. Spread on the baking sheet, leaving space between the cubes. Roast in the oven until tender and caramelized, about 40 minutes, tossing with a spatula every 10 to 15 minutes. Toast the almonds on a baking sheet in the same oven until they start to smell nutty, tossing once, about 10 minutes. Let cool.

3 In a large mixing bowl, toss the kale with the almonds, cheddar, and squash. Season to taste with lemon juice and olive oil (using about 1 tablespoon lemon juice and 2 tablespoons oil). Season to taste with salt and pepper.

4 Divide the salad between two plates or shallow bowls. Garnish with shaved Pecorino cheese and serve.

# Green Peach Salad

## FROM CROOK'S CORNER

When you get ahold of a perfectly ripe peach—soft, sweet, and ready to pour peach juice all over your shirt—you know what to do: Eat it right then and there, maybe even leaning over a trash can at the farmers' market. But for those bum peaches—the ones that could roll around the bottom of your bag all day and emerge unscathed—Bill Smith, longtime chef at Crook's Corner in Chapel Hill, gives us a low-maintenance salad that's perfect for the hottest, most beastly days of summer.

Green peaches, unless you have access to a peach orchard, are not actually green. Just poke around for the hardest, most unforgiving peaches in the pile. Unfortunately, these are easy to find, especially at your local grocery store. Once you shake some sugar and salt over some peach wedges and let them macerate for a mere 10 minutes, they'll turn glossy and bright as moisture is drawn out. A bit of peachy nectar collects in the bottom of the bowl, which you swish together with olive oil, mint, and lots of black pepper to make the dressing.

Bill Smith says this salad is great with cold meats. I think a big bowlful would make a lot of sense at either a hot, smoky barbecue or a civilized brunch.

### Serves 4 to 6

2½ pounds (1.1kg) unripe peaches, peeled and sliced as for pie into ½-inch (1.3cm) segments

Scant ¼ cup (50g) sugar

½ teaspoon salt

½ teaspoon freshly ground black pepper

2 tablespoons strong-flavored extra-virgin olive oil, like Greek or Lebanese

2 tablespoons chiffonade of fresh mint (see Genius Tips below)

1 Toss the peaches with the sugar and salt. Let them sit for 10 minutes. Fold in the pepper, oil, and mint. Serve immediately at room temperature or cold within a few hours of preparation; it will become mushy overnight.

### GENIUS TIPS

Hard green peaches will cling like the dickens to the pit, so I find it easiest to segment them before pitting—halving, then prying off one wedge at a time. Ripe peaches would cave and turn to pulp under such pressure, but green peaches maintain their dignity.

To chiffonade fresh mint (or any delicate, leafy herbs or greens), stack the leaves, with the largest ones on the bottom, roll the lot into a tight cylinder, and then slice it thinly crosswise. This will help you get a cleaner slice and will bruise the leaves less than going at them more roughly with a chef's knife.

# Red Salad

FROM FERGUS HENDERSON

All winter, we know that more colorful fruits and vegetables are on the way—the glowing greens of spring will be followed quickly by a red-hot riot of tomatoes and berries come summer. I don't mean to take away from those special times we have with sunnier ingredients, but here's a salad for the barren times—a red salad to rival any you'd see in July.

You could argue that any salad with beets becomes a red salad, but this one from chef Fergus Henderson is deliberate and quite clever about it. You'll stir together snippets of raw beet, purple cabbage, and red onion (to mellow the bite of the red onion, see tip on page 70) with balsamic vinegar, olive oil, and salty capers. What wasn't already red is instantly stained. Then you plate a heap of it next to some crème fraîche (or strained yogurt) and chervil (or curly parsley if you—like me—don't know where the hell to find chervil).

It's earthy, tangy, and sweet, like a borscht that makes you want to tear into your next course rather than go curl up in a warm place. The genius of this recipe is only enhanced by Henderson's fanciful writing style—it's inexact, but a salad doesn't really need rigor.

**Serves 6**

DRESSING

Healthy splashes of extra-virgin olive oil
A little gesture of balsamic vinegar
A small handful of extra-fine capers
Sea salt and freshly ground black pepper

2 raw beets, peeled and finely grated
¼ red cabbage, with its core cut out, very finely sliced
1 very small red onion, peeled, cut in half from top to bottom and finely sliced
6 healthy dollops of crème fraîche
2 healthy bunches of chervil (or curly parsley), stems discarded

1 Mix everything together for the dressing. Toss all your raw red vegetables in the dressing, taste and adjust seasoning, then on six plates place a bushel of this red mixture. Next to this, nustle your blob of crème fraîche as if the two ingredients were good friends, not on top of each other as if they were lovers. Finally a clump of the chervil rested next to the other ingredients in the friendly fashion. A very striking salad ready for the eater to mess up.

# Wild & White Rice Salad

## FROM VIANA LA PLACE & EVAN KLEIMAN

These days, we're leaning more on grain salads in our day-to-day cooking, for all kinds of good reasons: They make a sturdy brown bag lunch that's friendly to adaptation, more robust and filling than green salad, and more exciting than a big pot of brown rice. They do the work of carb and vegetable (and sometimes even protein) at once.

Now may be a good time to take a step back, to 1985, when Viana La Place and Evan Kleiman wrote *Cucina Fresca*—a book all about simple Italian foods that taste best at room temperature, a bible for make-ahead lunches (and dinners) and stressless picnic and party foods. This book, and this recipe in particular, are among the first that co-owner Matt Sartwell recommends at Kitchen Arts & Letters when customers are looking for cookbooks to improve their routines.

La Place and Kleiman's style of cooking has ridden out decades of trends by keeping it simple. In the case of this salad, for example, rely first on the grains—two kinds of rice. Cook them in two pots to give them both space, neither dragging the other down if you mistime or misunderstand them. Let them cool. What comes next is just a few utterly modest brightening agents (celery, parsley, red onion, oil, and vinegar). It needs nothing else. Don't go rummaging in the fridge—once you start adding, you'll tip the balance, and only then will you risk its tasting inadequate.

**Serves 6 to 8**

1 cup (185g) long-grain white rice
1 cup (160g) wild rice
½ small red onion, minced
3 celery stalks, peeled and minced
¼ cup (15g) minced fresh parsley

### DRESSING
½ cup (120ml) vegetable oil
2 tablespoons olive oil
¼ cup (60ml) balsamic vinegar or red wine vinegar
2 to 3 teaspoons Dijon mustard
Coarse salt and freshly ground black pepper

1 If using basmati rice, rinse it in several changes of water before cooking. Cook the rices separately in abundant amounts of salted boiling water until the grains are tender yet firm to the bite, 7 to 10 minutes for the white rice and 30 to 40 minutes for the wild rice. Drain the cooked rice into a large sieve and run cold water over the rice until the grains feel cool to the touch. Drain the rice thoroughly. Mix with the onion, celery, and parsley in a large bowl.

2 **To make the dressing,** combine the vegetable oil, olive oil, vinegar, and mustard in a small bowl. Pour over the rice mixture. Toss thoroughly to mix. Add salt and pepper to taste. Rice salad will generally keep for up 4 days, covered, in the refrigerator.

# Roasted Carrot & Avocado Salad with Crunchy Seeds

FROM ABC KITCHEN

Roasted carrots seem like a perfect realization of everything a carrot should be: their blunt crunch softened, their sweetness concentrated, their smooth facade pleasantly crinkled. In practice, though, they can have a hard time living up to their promise: They don't cook through, they burn, they somehow wind up flavorless. This recipe, from ABC Kitchen restaurant in New York City, does away with all of that.

By boiling the carrots in salted water first, briefly, while you put together their garlic-thyme-cumin marinade, they'll roast much more quickly, and nothing will burn. You'll also put half an orange and half a lemon in the roasting pan with them and use juices from the roasted citrus for the dressing. With this simple move, the dressing takes on a new dimension—mellow, sweet acid layered on bright. Construct your salad: your perfectly roasted carrots, wedges of avocado, a bramble of sprouts and herbs, crème fraîche, and citrusy dressing, sunflower and sesame seeds skittered all over.

### Serves 4

2 pounds (900g) small carrots (3 inches/7.5cm long and ½ inch/1.3cm thick) or large carrots, peeled, quartered, and cut into 3-inch (7.5cm) segments (about 4 cups/950ml)

Kosher salt

1 orange, one half juiced, the other left whole

1 lemon, one half juiced, the other left whole

½ cup (120ml) extra-virgin olive oil

1 teaspoon cumin seeds

2 medium cloves garlic

1 tablespoon fresh thyme leaves

1 teaspoon red wine vinegar

1 teaspoon crushed red pepper flakes

Freshly ground black pepper

1 tablespoon sugar

1 avocado, peeled and cut into 12 wedges

2 cups (about 60g) mixed baby sprouts, herbs, and microgreens

¼ cup (60g) crème fraîche

2 tablespoons toasted sunflower seeds

2 teaspoons toasted sesame seeds

1 Preheat the oven to 450°F (230°C) with an oven rack in the center.

2 Place the carrots in a saucepan and cover them with cold water. Season the water with a few pinches of salt, set the pan over high heat, and bring to a simmer. Reduce the heat to medium and simmer until the carrots are tender, about 10 minutes. Drain the carrots and transfer them to a rimmed baking sheet.

3 Combine 1 teaspoon each of the orange and lemon juices, 2 tablespoons of olive oil, the cumin, garlic, thyme, vinegar, and red pepper flakes in a blender and blend until smooth. Season the marinade to taste with salt and pepper. Add the marinade and the unjuiced citrus halves to the carrots and toss with your hands until evenly combined. Roast until the carrots are slightly shriveled with a few brown spots, about 20 minutes, tossing occasionally with a spatula to brown them evenly. Allow the carrots to cool to room temperature.

4 Once they've cooled slightly, squeeze the juice from the roasted citrus halves into a small bowl. Add the remaining fresh citrus juices, remaining 6 tablespoons (90ml) olive oil, and the sugar. Season the dressing to taste with salt and pepper and whisk to combine.

5 Divide the carrots and avocado slices among four plates and top with the greens. Add 1 tablespoon of crème fraîche to each salad. Sprinkle sunflower seeds and sesame seeds over each plate. Drizzle several tablespoons of the dressing over and around each salad (reserve any remaining dressing for another use) and serve immediately.

# Chickpea Stew with Saffron, Yogurt & Garlic

FROM HEIDI SWANSON

Despite its sturdy-sounding name, this chickpea stew has more in common with a summery Greek avgo-lemono than a fortifying Moroccan tagine. It comes from blogger and cookbook author Heidi Swanson and, like all of her recipes, feels revitalizing and pure without careening into asceticism.

Swanson lays the subtle flavor of saffron on a canvas of chickpeas and broth barely thickened with yogurt and a few egg yolks. If you've ever made a complicated paella and been uncertain what the saffron tastes like and why you paid good money for it, you'll find the answer in this stew. There it is!

The tempering stage of the recipe may sound stressful and dinner-risking, but it's actually very forgiving—and a trick you can use to enrich any number of soups. Just whisk a little hot stock into the yogurt, egg, and saffron mix, then whisk it back into the pot. What just looked anemic will suddenly turn creamy and gold. After this point, you're not supposed to let the soup come back to a boil—but at least once, in a distracted moment, I did, with no unpleasant side effects. (Full disclosure: In that instance, I was using full-fat yogurt. Lower-fat yogurt fans, I don't know if I can vouch for your chances.)

Serves 4 to 6

2 tablespoons extra-virgin olive oil
1 large yellow onion, finely chopped
Fine sea salt
3 cups (490g) cooked chickpeas or 2 (15-ounce/425g) cans chickpeas, rinsed and drained
4 cups (950ml) vegetable broth or water
2 cloves garlic, finely chopped
Scant ¼ teaspoon saffron threads (2 modest pinches)
3 large egg yolks, lightly beaten
1 cup (225g) plain yogurt (Greek or regular)
Sweet paprika
Small bunch fresh cilantro, chopped

1  In a medium-large pot over medium-high heat, combine the oil, onion, and a couple of big pinches of salt. Cook until the onions soften up a bit, a few minutes. Stir in the chickpeas, then add the vegetable broth and garlic. Bring to a simmer and remove from the heat.

2  In a bowl, whisk together the saffron and egg yolks, then whisk in the yogurt. Slowly add a big ladleful, at least 1 cup (240ml), of the hot broth to the yogurt mixture, stirring constantly. Very slowly whisk this mixture back into the pot of soup. Return the pot to medium heat and cook, stirring continuously and never quite allowing the broth to simmer for another 5 minutes or so, until the broth thickens slightly.

3  Ladle into individual bowls and serve sprinkled with a touch of paprika and plenty of chopped cilantro.

# Spicy Tomato Soup

FROM BARBARA LYNCH

You can make this spicy tomato soup from chef Barbara Lynch on a whim and eat it nearly as soon. It's also, at its core, six vegan ingredients you probably already have.

It's a drinkable broth with a big personality that's especially welcome in the midst of winter, when we don't expect loud colors in our diet, or food that makes our blood run hot. The fast-paced technique is also a good break from our wintry tendencies to hunker down for long stretches in the kitchen—to cook meats until they fall apart and Crock-Pot things. It's also great with a grilled cheese (page 166).

The recipe starts a bit like the old just-add-water canned tomato soup but quickly veers off and tastes like living, breathing fruit instead of tomato ghosts in corn syrup. In almost no time, you come out with a full-flavored soup, racy and pure. Lynch says the rustic pulp that's left behind after straining has no place here—you don't have to agree, or you can save the remains for crostini, pasta, or eggs.

Serves 6

2 tablespoons extra-virgin olive oil

1 small yellow onion, peeled, halved, and sliced into ¼-inch (6mm) thick slices

1 teaspoon crushed red pepper flakes (or start with ½ teaspoon)

2 (28-ounce/800g) cans whole tomatoes

1½ cups (360ml) water

¼ cup (6g) loosely packed fresh basil leaves

Kosher salt and freshly ground black pepper

Crème fraîche, for garnish (optional)

1 Heat the olive oil in a large saucepan over medium heat until shimmering. Add the onion and red pepper flakes and cook, stirring occasionally, until the onions are translucent and very tender, about 10 minutes.

2 Stir in the tomatoes and their juices, plus the water, and bring to a boil. Reduce the heat to low and simmer, stirring occasionally, until the flavors have melded, about 30 minutes. (If you're in a hurry, you can skip the simmer time—just add a bit less water.) Add the basil, season with salt and pepper, remove from the heat, and let cool briefly, about 5 minutes.

3 Set a fine-mesh strainer over a large, heatproof bowl. Using a blender, puree the soup in batches until smooth, removing the small cap from the blender lid (the pour lid) and covering the space with a kitchen towel (this allows steam from the hot soup to escape and prevents the blender lid from popping off). Pour the blended soup through the strainer, pressing on the solids with a rubber spatula or ladle; discard the solids. Taste the soup and season with additional salt and pepper as needed.

4 Return the soup to the saucepan and reheat on medium-low until hot. If you choose, serve topped with a tablespoon of crème fraîche.

# Cauliflower Soup

## FROM PAUL BERTOLLI

This recipe will tell you to put a cauliflower and an onion in a pot, add water, then add water . . . then add some more water. You probably want to put down the cookbook and wander away looking for a cheeseburger, right? It sounds downright grim, but Paul Bertolli, who was at the helm of Chez Panisse and Oliveto for more than twenty years, knows exactly how to make a vegetable become the best it can be. His formula for cauliflower soup is precise to the ounce and simple to follow, even with a raised eyebrow. (Seriously, more water?) With a little boiling and swirling in a blender, the cauliflower puts up no resistance—the vegetable's natural pectin is enough to make it creamy, without any added dairy.

It's tempting to add crème fraîche or bacon, *vadouvan*, or a thick lump of butter—trust me, all of them would be delicious—but I encourage you to not add a thing. When you curb your instincts to overseason and over-fatten, yes, sometimes you end up with gruel—but sometimes you get a supple, magical puree that's delicate and sweet and smooth as a flannel scarf. Even if you're not a fan of cauliflower (Bertolli isn't), make an exception for this soup.

**Serves 8**

3 tablespoons olive oil

1 medium onion (6 ounces/170g), sliced thin

1 pound 6 ounces (625g) very fresh cauliflower, broken into florets

Salt

5½ cups (1.3L) hot water

Extra-virgin olive oil

Freshly ground black pepper

1 Warm the olive oil in a heavy-bottomed pot. Sweat the onion in the olive oil over low heat without letting it brown for 15 minutes.

2 Add the cauliflower, salt to taste, and ½ cup (120ml) of the water. Raise the heat slightly, and cover the pot tightly. Stew the cauliflower for 15 to 18 minutes, or until tender. Then add another 4½ cups (1L) of hot water, bring to a low simmer, and cook an additional 20 minutes.

3 Working in batches, puree the soup in a blender to a very smooth, creamy consistency. Let the soup stand for 20 minutes. In this time it will thicken slightly.

4 Thin the soup with the remaining ½ cup (120ml) hot water. Reheat the soup. Serve hot, drizzled with a thin stream of extra-virgin olive oil and freshly ground black pepper.

"Add cream or seasonings such as curry (a common cure) to cauliflower, or add solid garnishes, and you steal from it." —P.B.

# Potato Soup with Fried Almonds

### FROM ANYA VON BREMZEN

Anya von Bremzen's potato soup from *The New Spanish Table* is sharper than your average chowder or vichyssoise because its substance doesn't come from cream or flour, but rather from almonds, toasted in garlicky olive oil and ground. About half the potatoes melt into the broth, the rest are left in ragged chunks. A bit of diced Serrano ham (or prosciutto) and a pinch of saffron go a long way, adding a luxurious gloss to what is otherwise a peasant stew.

If this sounds too rich and savory, remember that you'll have held back a handful of ground almonds and splashed them with some sherry vinegar just before serving, making a soup that's cozy but bright in every spoonful.

Those almond bits that have been simmering with the soup for the duration are softened and plumped; the last-minute ones a still-crunchy carrier for the vinegar. The potatoes, like butter. If you wanted an unobstructed, smooth soup, this isn't it.

### Serves 4 as an appetizer

1½ pounds (680g) Yukon Gold potatoes

¼ cup (60ml) extra-virgin olive oil

½ cup (75g) whole blanched almonds

6 large cloves garlic, peeled

⅓ cup (about 2 ounces/55g) finely diced Serrano ham or prosciutto

4 cups (950ml) chicken stock (page 92), or more if needed

Coarse salt and freshly ground black pepper

Pinch of saffron, crushed

2 teaspoons sherry vinegar, preferably aged, or more to taste

2 tablespoons minced fresh flat-leaf parsley

Dense country bread, for serving

1 Cut the potatoes into irregular chunks by inserting the tip of a small, sharp knife into a potato and twisting until a 1½-inch (4cm) chunk comes out. Repeat until the entire potato is cut up, then continue with the remaining potatoes; set aside. Alternatively, coarsely chop the potatoes into 1½-inch (4cm) chunks. Peeling is optional.

2 Heat the oil in a heavy 3-quart (2.8L) saucepan over medium heat. Add the almonds and garlic and cook, stirring, until golden, 4 to 5 minutes, adjusting the heat so the oil doesn't burn. Using a slotted spoon, transfer the almonds and garlic to a bowl to cool slightly. Add the ham to the pan and stir for 1 minute. Add the potatoes and cook, stirring, for another minute. Add the chicken stock and bring to a boil, skimming off any foam that rises to the surface. Reduce the heat to medium-low and simmer the soup.

3 Meanwhile, place the almond and garlic mixture in a food processor and grind it. If you like almond bits in your soup, grind the mixture somewhat coarsely; otherwise, grind it finely. Add all but about 2 tablespoons to the soup. Season with salt and pepper to taste.

4 Steep the saffron in a few tablespoons of the soup broth for 2 minutes, then add it to the soup. Simmer the soup, partially covered, until about half the potatoes have disintegrated, about 35 minutes. Skim the soup as it cooks if you like, and add a little more stock if the soup seems too thick.

5 When you are ready to serve, check the texture of the soup. If you'd like it creamier, break up some of the potatoes with a sturdy spoon. Add the vinegar to the reserved ground almond mixture and stir it into the soup. Add the parsley and cook for a minute. Taste for seasoning, adding a little more vinegar, if needed. Serve the soup with bread.

# More Genius for Soups & Salads

## Cheese Brodo

ADAPTED FROM NATE APPLEMAN

You might have heard of tossing a spent Parmesan rind into your minestrone as it simmers. Some grocery stores have even gotten wise and started selling their rinds by the pound. But when it's time to make soup, it's easy to forget the stash of rinds in your cheese drawer or freezer.

Next time you bump into them and kick yourself for all your cheeseless soups, make *brodo* (Italian for broth), which you can use as a flavorful base for any soup, stew, or risotto. Just simmer your rinds in water—even small amounts of rind will give you a rich, already-seasoned broth. Nate Appleman's bare-bones version uses 6 ounces (170g) cheese rinds to 2 quarts (1.9L) of water, and a bay leaf, simmered for 1½ hours. Note that it's not vegetarian in the strictest sense, because of rennet used in the Parmesan production. Makes 3 cups (710ml) and will keep, tightly sealed in the fridge, for a week. It also freezes well for up to 3 months.

## Lemon Salt

ADAPTED FROM PATRICIA WELLS

Grinding up your own lemon salt frees all the fragrant oils in the zest and spreads them around to travel with the salt—farther than they could of their own accord. I first encountered this seasoning trick in Patricia Wells's zucchini carpaccio with avocado, thyme, and pistachios—and it will perk up any salad. Or swirl it into buttered pasta, dust it on blanched green beans, put a pinch on a dark chocolate cookie.

Combine equal parts of lemon zest and fine sea salt, grind it in a spice grinder, and store it in the refrigerator tightly sealed in a jar for up to 1 week, after which the flavor begins to fade.

## Chicken Stock

ADAPTED FROM TOM COLICCHIO

If you thought you were supposed to make chicken stock by simmering bones, vegetables, and herbs in water for a long time, that's partially true. Yes, the bones should gently simmer for about 3 hours. But if you add the vegetables and herbs at the same time, nothing fresh will be left by the end.

To make 5 cups (1.2L) of Tom Colicchio's well-layered stock, put 4 pounds of chicken bones (backs and necks work well) and cold water to cover in a pot and simmer for 2½ hours, skimming as needed, until the stock tastes like chicken. Then add 1 onion, 1 carrot, 2 celery ribs, and the white parts of 2 leeks, all chopped coarsely, and keep simmering for 30 minutes. Add 3 to 4 sprigs each of thyme and parsley only for the last 10 minutes. Strain and keep tightly covered in the fridge for up to a week (spooning off the top layer of fat once it's cool, if you like), or freeze for up to 6 months.

## Red Wine Vinaigrette

ADAPTED FROM MOLLY WIZENBERG
& BRANDON PETTIT

You can make any old vinegar taste fancy, with just a splash of red wine—a hack from Molly Wizenberg and Brandon Pettit of Seattle's Delancey restaurant (and blog *Orangette*). Pettit discovered this trick after he ran out of homemade vinegar and store brands didn't live up. A little red wine rounds out the rough edges, "making up for imperfections in your vinegar," as Wizenberg writes.

Stir together 2 tablespoons Dijon mustard (preferably Roland Extra Strong, Beaufor, or Edmond Fallot), 1½ tablespoons red wine vinegar, 2 teaspoons red wine, and a pinch of fine sea salt and of sugar, then slowly whisk in ¼ cup (60ml) olive oil. The dressing should look opaque and somewhat creamy, almost peachy in color. Makes about ½ cup (120ml) and will keep in the fridge indefinitely.

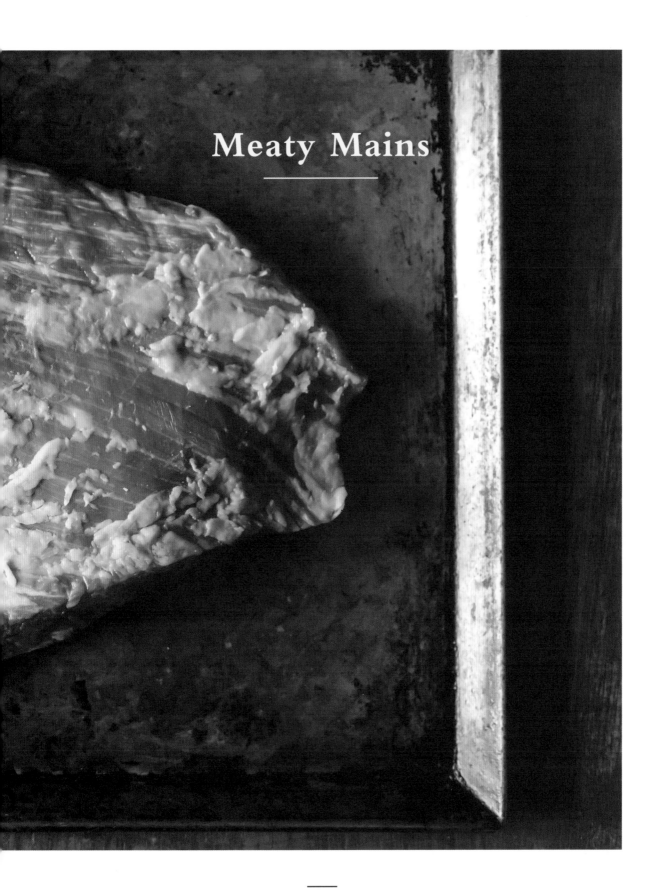

# Meaty Mains

# Salt-Baked Herbed Salmon with Red Onion-Caper Vinaigrette

## FROM CORY SCHREIBER

Perfectly seared salmon is a beautiful accomplishment, but that doesn't mean you always want to be doing it. Not when there's a method that takes the precision out of your concern, that keeps the stovetop clean and tidy, that scales up considerably better than searing fillets one by one or two by two.

To guarantee the fish cooks gently, chef Cory Schreiber bakes it on a bed of rock salt to diffuse the heat (it also helps season the fillets through the skin). And so that we're not disappointed when we see pale pink salmon instead of a shiny brown crust, he cakes fresh herbs on top where they'll stay green and pretty. Then he serves it with a vinegary red onion and caper dressing to ensure no scraps of salmon are left behind. This recipe halves well, but there's no harm in making extra: Both salmon and vinaigrette are excellent cold the next day for lunch.

Serves 8

### VINAIGRETTE

1 cup (240ml) olive oil

¼ cup (60ml) sherry vinegar

1 teaspoon Dijon mustard

1 red onion, thinly sliced

2 teaspoons capers, drained

1 teaspoon chopped fresh basil

1 teaspoon fine sea salt

¾ teaspoon freshly ground black pepper

### SALMON

4 pounds (1.8kg) salmon fillet, pinbones removed, with skin intact

2 tablespoons mixed minced fresh herbs, such as tarragon, basil, flat-leaf parsley, and thyme

2 tablespoons fennel seeds, cracked

1 teaspoon fine sea salt

½ teaspoon freshly ground black pepper

Rock salt or kosher salt, for lining pan

1 **To prepare the vinaigrette,** in a small bowl, whisk together the oil, vinegar, and mustard. Stir in the onion, capers, basil, salt, and pepper. Cover and refrigerate until you are ready to serve. The vinaigrette can be made up to 2 days ahead.

2 **To prepare the salmon,** rub the fillet with the minced herbs and fennel seeds. Season with salt and pepper. At this point, the salmon can be covered and refrigerated overnight.

3 Preheat the oven to 325°F (165°C). Cover a large sheet pan or roasting pan with aluminum foil. Pour the rock or kosher salt into the pan, covering its surface. Place the salmon, skin side down, on the salt.

4 Bake for 35 to 45 minutes, or until the fish is opaque on the outside and slightly translucent in the center. This method of cooking allows the salmon to cook through without becoming dry. Remove from the oven, cover loosely with aluminum foil, and let stand for 5 minutes (the salmon will continue to cook).

5 To serve, use a wide spatula to remove the salmon from the salt. Remove the skin and portion the salmon onto plates. Spoon some of the vinaigrette over each portion and serve.

---

### GENIUS TIPS

If you can't find rock salt or another coarse salt, this technique works with finer salts, but the skin will be too salty to eat—just be careful not to tip the fish over and get any on the flesh. You can also add aromatic whole spices like star anise and cinnamon to the salt, a trick learned from cookbook author Lora Zarubin.

# Shrimp Grits

## FROM EDNA LEWIS & SCOTT PEACOCK

Edna Lewis and Scott Peacock met in 1988 when she was seventy-three and he was twenty-six. They became best friends and cooking partners, wrote a cookbook together in 2003, and lived together for the last six years of her life.

The first time Peacock remembers making this dish was for Lewis's 75th birthday party, in tiny cocktail party portions, with a dollop of Lewis's sherried fresh shrimp paste hovering on top of his creamy grits. But over the years they cooked together, the recipe evolved. They realized that the shrimp paste and grits, when stirred together completely and left to rest for a few minutes, became something even more beguiling. "Just give them a moment to get to know each other," Peacock explains. "You don't want them to be strangers."

You might wonder why you'd want to put something as delicate as shrimp in a food processor. But they whip up into a puree that's very good on crackers and as an all-purpose flavor enhancer (just imagine folding some into risotto, saucing fish, or filling tea sandwiches with it). And most importantly, stirred through grits, shrimp paste goes further than a few prawns piled on top ever could, filling every spoonful with buttery, boozy shrimp at its best and most seductive.

**Serves 4 to 6**

### SHRIMP PASTE
1 cup (230g) unsalted butter, plus more as needed
1 pound (450g) fresh shrimp, peeled, tails removed, and deveined (Peacock likes small, sweet ones like Gulf shrimp, but get whatever is freshest)
½ teaspoon salt
½ teaspoon freshly ground black pepper
¼ cup (60ml) sherry
2 tablespoons fresh lemon juice
¼ teaspoon cayenne pepper

### GRITS
2 cups (475ml) water, plus more as needed
2 cups (475ml) milk, plus more as needed
1 cup (155g) stone-ground or regular grits
¼ cup (60ml) heavy cream
2 tablespoons unsalted butter
Kosher salt
Chives (optional)

1 **To make the shrimp paste,** heat 6 tablespoons (85g) of the butter in a large skillet until it is hot and foaming. Add the shrimp, salt, and pepper, and cook over high heat, stirring often, for 4 to 7 minutes, until the shrimp are pink and cooked through. Remove the skillet from the stove and use a slotted spoon to transfer the cooked shrimp to the bowl of a food processor with the blade attachment.

2 Return the skillet to the stove and add the sherry, lemon juice, and cayenne. Cook over high heat until the liquid in the skillet is reduced to approximately 3 tablespoons and is quite syrupy. Immediately add this to the shrimp in the food processor and process until the shrimp are thoroughly pureed. With the motor running, add the remaining 10 tablespoons (145g) butter in pieces and process until thoroughly blended. Turn the food processor off and carefully taste the paste for seasoning, adding more salt, black pepper, sherry, lemon juice, or cayenne as needed. Transfer the shrimp paste to a ceramic crock and allow to cool completely.

3 If not using right away, cover the shrimp paste and refrigerate for up to 1 week. Refrigerated shrimp paste should be allowed to return to room temperature before serving. If it is too dry to spread, you may work in some softened butter and salt to taste until it is spreadable.

4 **To make the grits,** heat the water and milk in a heavy-bottomed saucepan until just simmering. While the milk and water are heating, put the grits in a large mixing bowl and cover with cool water. (If you are using regular grits, skip this step.) Stir the grits assertively so that the chaff floats to the top. Carefully skim the surface of the grits to remove the chaff. Drain the grits through a fine strainer, and stir them into the simmering water and milk. Cook, stirring often, until the grits are tender to the bite and have thickened to the consistency of thick oatmeal. Regular grits are done in about 20 minutes, but stone-ground grits require an hour or a little more to cook, and you will have to add additional milk and water as needed. As the grits thicken, stir them more often to keep them from sticking and scorching.

5 Stir in the cream and butter and season generously with salt to taste. Remove from the heat and let rest, covered, until it is time to serve. If the grits become too thick as they cool, reheat them, stirring in a little extra boiling water or hot milk to thin.

6 To serve, top the hot grits with a generous dollop of the shrimp paste. Scott Peacock likes to stir it in thoroughly, then let it rest for 5 to 10 minutes. For every cup (240ml) of grits, stir in about ¼ cup (60ml) or more of the shrimp paste, and sprinkle some chopped fresh chives on top, if you like them. Serve as an appetizer, a supper dish with buttered toast, or a savory side dish.

# Crispy-Skinned Fish

## FROM LE BERNARDIN

In the carnival of high technique at Le Bernardin, there are many dishes you'd never try to re-create. But the cooks on the line use a surprisingly simple method to get seared fish with a taut, golden skin that won't get pushed to the side of the plate.

The secret is Wondra flour, usually heralded for its use in clumpless gravies and sauces. It's known more generically as instant flour, because it's been pre-cooked and dried using a "patented agglomeration process," which leaves it with a fine, slightly gritty texture reminiscent of cornmeal. Some malted barley flour is thrown in, too. All of this means that it's more prone to beautiful browning and crisping than regular all-purpose flour.

Despite its scary casserole-era packaging, it turns out that Wondra has long been a favorite of Julia Child (for crepe batter), Jacques Pépin (for chicken cutlets), David Bouley (for dusting anything pan-fried), and Le Bernardin's gleaming star chef, Eric Ripert. Ripert has been known to use Wondra on everything from monkfish loins to soft-shell crab, but it's especially good for bringing out the beauty of skin-on fillets of fish like salmon or striped bass.

**Serves 4**

About 1 tablespoon canola oil (enough to coat the bottom of the pan)

4 (6-ounce/170g) skin-on fish fillets (like striped bass or salmon)

Fine sea salt

Freshly ground white pepper (black is fine too, if you don't mind the speckles)

Wondra flour, for dusting

1 Preheat the oven to 400°F (200°C).

2 Heat the oil in a large oven- and flame-proof sauté pan on the stovetop until the oil is very hot, but not smoking.

3 Season the fish on both sides with salt and pepper and dust with Wondra flour. Blow off the excess. Put the fish in the pan, skin side down, and press down on the fish with a spatula. (The skin immediately contracts and buckles, but you want to keep it all in contact with the pan for maximum crisping.) Sear on the stovetop over medium heat until golden brown on the bottom, about 3 minutes.

4 Turn the fish over, put the pan in the oven, and roast for another 2 to 3 minutes, until a metal skewer can be easily inserted into the center of the fillet and, if left for 5 seconds, feels just warm when touched to your lip. Serve immediately.

# Rosemary-Brined Buttermilk Fried Chicken

FROM MICHAEL RUHLMAN

If you love fried chicken but would sooner wait for a road trip to Mississippi than get frying yourself, what you need is a recipe that won't fail you, comes together swiftly, and is more than worth what little trouble it asks of you.

Here, you'll brine the chicken, which is extra insurance for keeping the meat flavorful and moist, and it will take you 15 minutes to go from chicken in grocery bag to chicken brining in the fridge.

How? Namely, how do four cloves of garlic and a whole sliced onion go into a pot over medium-high heat with *1 teaspoon* of oil and quickly sweat into a soft puddle, without browning (or burning)?

The answer: a lot of salt. It instantly goes to work on the onions, drawing out their moisture, which pools in the bottom of the pot and helps it all quickly cook down in its own juices. Then you toss in rosemary branches and finish it off with water and lemon. Boil, ice bath, throw your chicken in it. The next day (or even just a few hours later), you'll pull your chicken out of the brine, which will smell confusingly delicious, and you'll start dredging and frying.

The seasoned flour and buttermilk crust is one of those shaggy, crunchy affairs that you'd normally want to steal off other people's drumsticks and leave them the meat lingering on the bone. But remember that brine: As intoxicating as it smelled before cooking, it will smell—and taste—even more richly of rosemary and lemon, the salt having drawn it into the flesh.

The meat is so juicy, the crust so proudly crusty, you can fry it ahead and leave it in the oven until company arrives. (Have you ever tried to deep-fry chicken while guests are standing around drinking? They ask an awful lot of questions.) Best keep them away till the big reveal.

## Serves 6 to 8

### BRINE
1 small onion, thinly sliced

4 cloves garlic, smashed with the flat side of a knife

1 teaspoon vegetable oil

3 tablespoons kosher salt

5 to 6 branches rosemary, each 4 to 5 inches (10 to 13cm) long

4½ cups (1L) water

1 lemon, halved

8 chicken legs, drumsticks and thighs separated

8 chicken wings, wing tips removed

3 cups (420g) all-purpose flour

3 tablespoons freshly ground black pepper

2 tablespoons sweet paprika

2 tablespoons fine sea salt

2 teaspoons cayenne pepper

2 tablespoons baking powder

2 cups (475ml) buttermilk

Neutral, high-heat oil for deep-frying (such as canola)

Rosemary spigs (to deep fry) and lemon zest, for garnish

**1** **To make the brine,** in a saucepan over medium-high heat, sauté the onion and garlic in the oil until translucent, 3 to 4 minutes. Add the kosher salt after the onion and garlic have cooked for 30 seconds or so. Add the rosemary and cook to heat it, 30 seconds or so. Add the water and lemon, squeezing the juice into the water and removing any seeds. Bring the water to a simmer, stirring to dissolve the salt. Remove from the heat and allow the brine to cool. Refrigerate until chilled. To speed this process up, chill over an ice bath, stirring.

**2** Place all the chicken pieces in a large, sturdy plastic bag. Set the bag in a large bowl for support. Pour the cooled brine and aromatics into the bag. Seal the bag

CONTINUED

# Rosemary-Brined Buttermilk Fried Chicken
## Continued

so that you remove as much air as possible and the chicken is submerged in the brine. Refrigerate for at least 8 hours, and up to 24 hours, agitating the bag occasionally to redistribute the brine and the chicken.

3 Remove the chicken from the brine, rinse under cold water, pat dry, and set on a rack or on paper towels. The chicken can be refrigerated for up to 3 days before you cook it, or it can be cooked immediately. Ideally, it should be refrigerated, uncovered, for a day to dry out the skin, but Ruhlman says he usually can't wait to start cooking.

4 Combine the flour, black pepper, paprika, sea salt, cayenne, and baking powder in a bowl. Whisk to distribute the ingredients. Divide this mixture between two bowls. Pour the buttermilk into a third bowl. Set a rack on a baking sheet.

5 Dredge the chicken in the seasoned flour, shake off the excess, and set the dusted pieces on the rack. Dip the pieces in the buttermilk, then dredge them aggressively in the second bowl of seasoned flour and return them to the rack.

6 Heat the oil in a large, high-sided pot (Ruhlman recommends filling it no more than one-third full with oil) for deep-frying to 350°F (180°C). Add as many chicken pieces as you can without crowding the pan. Cook the chicken, turning the pieces occasionally, until they are golden brown and cooked through, 12 to 15 minutes depending on their size. Remove to a clean rack and allow them to rest for 5 to 10 minutes before serving. Fry the rosemary sprigs. When ready to serve, garnish with lemon zest and fried rosemary sprigs.

### GENIUS TIP

Happily, this is a great make-ahead dish; the chicken will keep well for a couple of hours. Fry it early, then keep it on a rack in a 250°F (120°C) oven until you need it. If you have a convection oven, use that feature to keep the crust crisp.

"This is the best fried chicken, ever. There, I said it. If it's not, then I want to try yours." —M.R.

# Simplest Roast Chicken

## FROM BARBARA KAFKA

The juiciest, speediest, most bewitchingly golden roast chicken also happens to be the one with the recipe you can remember without googling. Just 10 minutes a pound at 500°F (260°C). That's right, the whole time.

Today, it seems we want most everything singed and caramelized at 450°F (230°C) or higher, but in 1995 when Kafka wrote *Roasting: A Simple Art*, people were suspicious. Fewer foods were roasted then, and when they were, the standard oven temperatures ran 100°F (40°C) cooler.

Kafka changed that. For a while, her high-heat roast chicken was all the rage, but inevitably other techniques caught our attention—spatchcocking! vertical roasting! wet brining! dry brining!—and we moved on. For our any-night roast chicken, I recommend we briefly return to 1995. Why? Because there's no basting and no trussing. You needn't remember to turn the heat up or down after so many minutes; nor flip the creature awkwardly halfway through. There's no snipping of spines or slashing of limbs; no stuffing butter deep into loose corners of skin.

Just be sure to put it in the oven bum-first, so the slower-cooking legs are nearer the heat at the back of the oven. That's about it. As Kafka says: "If there is no lemon, garlic, or butter on hand, roast the chicken without them. Or play."

### Serves 2 to 4

One 5- to 6-pound (2.3 to 2.7kg) chicken, wing tips removed, brought to room temperature, if possible

1 lemon, halved (optional)

4 cloves garlic (optional)

¼ cup (60g) unsalted butter (optional)

Kosher salt and freshly ground black pepper

1 cup (240ml) chicken stock (page 92), water, fruit juice, or wine for optional deglazing

1 Preheat a regular oven to 500°F (260°C) or a convection oven to 450°F (230°C). Place an oven rack on the second level from the bottom of the oven.

2 Remove the fat from the tail and crop ends of the chicken. Freeze the neck and giblets for stock. Reserve the chicken liver for another use. Stuff the cavity of the chicken with the lemon, garlic, and butter, if using. Season the cavity and skin with salt and pepper.

3 Place the chicken in a 12 by 8 by 1½-inch (30 by 20 by 4cm) roasting pan breast side up. Put into the oven legs first and roast for 50 to 60 minutes, or until the juices run clear. After the first 10 minutes, move the chicken with a wooden spoon or spatula to keep it from sticking.

4 Remove the chicken to a platter by placing a large wooden spoon into the tail end and balancing the chicken with a kitchen spoon pressed against the crop end. As you lift the chicken, carefully tilt it over the roasting pan so that all the juices run out and into the pan.

5 To make a sauce from the pan juices, if one is desired, pour off or spoon out excess fat from the roasting pan and put the roasting pan on top of the stove. Add the stock or other liquid and bring the contents of the pan to a boil while scraping the bottom vigorously with a wooden spoon. Let reduce by half. Serve the sauce over the chicken or, for crisp skin, in a sauceboat.

**GENIUS TIP**

The single complaint I've heard about this recipe is that there can be too much spattering or smoke. Kafka advises (temporarily) unplugging your smoke detector and setting your oven to self-clean before bed. But another solution is to add roughly chopped potatoes or other hardy vegetables to the pan—they'll absorb the delicious juices from the chicken and keep them from spluttering. Stir them once or twice during roasting and, if they aren't cooked through or crisped enough when the chicken is done, simply return the pan to the oven (sans chicken) until they are, decreasing the temperature as needed.

# Chicken Thighs with Lemon

## FROM CANAL HOUSE

"Short of turning chicken on a spit over live wood embers, I know of no better process for cooking chicken, nor one that delivers more satisfying or true flavors," Paul Bertolli (see page 88) wrote of this technique, which he calls "bottom-up cooking," in *Cooking by Hand.*

You don't sear, and you don't roast, and you don't grill—you don't do any of the things we're taught to do to chicken. Instead, you lay the chicken, skin side down, in a barely hot pan. Then you leave it mostly alone for about 30 minutes, flipping only once. The skin becomes impossibly crisp, enough so to satisfy your darkest fried chicken cravings.

Bertolli's is a worthy technique to play with, but Melissa Hamilton and Christopher Hirsheimer of Canal House have streamlined it for us. They use only thighs, which lie flat, maximizing the crisping area, and jigsaw easily into a round skillet. Unlike Bertolli, they also allow for a bit of olive oil to get the process rolling.

The simplest version of the sauce has only a bit of minced-up preserved lemon stirred into the pan juices at the end, but you can play with this technique as you like. Hirsheimer and Hamilton suggest two more seasoning variations—sherry and mushrooms, or bacon and olives. You can deglaze and make a gravy or a fancy pan sauce. Or just eat all the chicken as fast as you can.

**Serves 4**

1 tablespoon olive oil
8 bone-in, skin-on chicken thighs
Salt and freshly ground black pepper
Rind from half a preserved lemon
Lemon wedges, for serving

1 Put the olive oil into a large, heavy skillet over medium heat. Season the chicken thighs with salt and pepper and add them to the skillet, skin side down. Cook them like this, without moving them, until the fat has rendered out and the skin is deep golden brown and crisp, 15 to 30 minutes. Fiddle with the heat, reducing it to medium-low if the skin begins to burn before it gets evenly golden brown. Turn the thighs over and stir the preserved lemon rind into the fat in the skillet. Continue cooking the thighs until the meat closest to the bone is cooked through, about 15 minutes more. Serve the thighs and lemony pan drippings with the lemon wedges.

# Dry-Brined Turkey (a.k.a. The Judy Bird)

FROM RUSS PARSONS

In 2006, the *Los Angeles Times*'s food section held a turkey taste test that changed the way we cook for Thanksgiving. The winning bird had been dry-brined (though the term "dry-brining" wasn't being tossed around yet). In less fancy words, a few tablespoons of salt had been sprinkled on it a few days ahead.

Food editor Russ Parsons had Zuni Café's Judy Rodgers to thank for the salting technique, so—although she never liked turkey much herself—he named this one after her. The Judy Bird was born. As Rodgers taught him, salting early doesn't dry food out—if timed and measured right, it pulls moisture out and back in again, and the process magically realigns the proteins so that they'll hold on tighter next time. What this means to your mouth is juicy, tender food—and a turkey that's much less likely to overcook and dry out. As a bonus, it's salted all the way to its middle, not just on the surface. And, unlike with wet brines, you don't need to find room in your fridge for a turkey-sized vat of liquid.

Parsons wrote about the salting technique for the next five years in a row, testing new variations each year and slashing steps he decided weren't important. By his count, he's received more than a thousand emails from happy cooks.

**Serves 11 to 15**

One 12- to 16-pound (5.4 to 7.3kg) turkey (frozen is fine)
Kosher salt (we used Diamond Crystal brand)
Herbs and/or spices to flavor the salt, such as smoked paprika and orange zest, bay leaf and thyme, or rosemary and lemon zest (optional)
Melted butter, for basting (optional)

1 Rinse the turkey inside and out, pat it dry and weigh it. Measure 1 tablespoon of salt into a bowl for every 5 pounds (2.3kg) the turkey weighs (for a 15-pound/6.8kg turkey, use 3 tablespoons). Flavor the salt with herbs and spices if you like. Grind them together in a spice grinder, small food processor, or mortar and pestle.

2 Sprinkle the inside of the turkey lightly with the salt. Place the turkey on its back and salt the breasts, concentrating the salt in the center, where the meat is thickest. You'll probably use a little more than a tablespoon. It should look liberally seasoned, but not oversalted. Turn the turkey on one side and sprinkle the entire side with salt, concentrating on the thigh. You should use a little less than a tablespoon. Flip the turkey over and do the same with the opposite side. Place the turkey in a 2½-gallon (9.5L) sealable plastic bag, press out the air, and seal tightly. (If you can't find a resealable bag this big, you can use a turkey oven bag, but be prepared for it to leak.) Place the turkey breast-side up in the refrigerator. Chill for 3 days, turning it onto its breast for the last day. Rub the salt around once a day if you remember. Liquid will collect in the bag—this is normal.

3 Remove the turkey from the bag. There should be no salt visible on the surface, and the skin should be moist but not wet. Place the turkey breast-side up on a plate and refrigerate uncovered for at least 8 hours.

CONTINUED

4 On the day it is to be cooked, remove the turkey from the refrigerator and leave it at room temperature for at least 1 hour. Preheat the oven to 425°F (220°C).

5 Pat the turkey dry one last time and baste with melted butter, if using. Place the turkey breast-side down on a roasting rack in a roasting pan; put it in the oven. After 30 minutes, remove the pan from the oven and carefully turn the turkey over so the breast is facing up (it's easiest to do this by hand, using kitchen towels or oven mitts).

6 Reduce the oven temperature to 325°F (165°C), return the turkey to the oven, and roast until a thermometer inserted in the deepest part of the thigh, but not touching the bone, reads 165°F (75°C), about 2¾ hours total roasting.

7 Remove the turkey from the oven, transfer it to a warm platter or carving board, and tent loosely with foil. Let stand for at least 30 minutes to allow the juices to redistribute through the meat. Carve and serve.

## Cranberry Sauce
ADAPTED FROM DANIEL HUMM

This uncooked, three-ingredient cranberry sauce is a little like the raw cran-orange relish your aunt brings to Thanksgiving every year. Except the cranberries, instead of settling into a homogenous slush in the food processor, spin for an hour on low in the stand mixer, softening just enough to make a bright, jewel-like compote (see opposite). (Don't use frozen cranberries for this—they'll break down too much.)

Combine 12 ounces (340g) of fresh cranberries, 12 ounces (about 1⅔ cups or 340g) of granulated sugar, and 2 teaspoons of grated orange zest in the bowl of a stand mixer fitted with a paddle attachment. Mix on the lowest speed for at least an hour, until the cranberries begin to break down. (If they're popping out of the bowl at the beginning, drape it with a clean kitchen towel.) Cover and refrigerate the sauce for at least a couple of hours and up to a couple of days. Serves 6.

# Onion Carbonara

FROM MICHEL RICHARD

Bacon (or guanciale), cheese, and egg make such a fine, creamy sauce together, we should be applying them to more than just pasta. A sheen of carbonara goes well on pizza, wilted greens—even steamed onions.

When chef Michel Richard devised this recipe, he planned it as a low-carb alternative to spaghetti (in case there were any question of his intentions, he called it "Low Carb-O-Nara"). But what he discovered was that steamed onion masquerading as pasta is really good for its own reasons entirely.

When you slice an onion into long ribbons and steam them, the ribbons taste clean and sweet, all their fire washed away. They'll also retain their form a bit better than if you were to sauté them, so you can neatly twirl them around a fork. It may seem fussy and wasteful to use only the longest loops you can extract from an onion, but you can use the remains for something else. Chicken stock (page 92) or pasta with yogurt and caramelized onions (page 144), perhaps.

---

"The larger lesson to take from all of this is that blanching onions, even diced onions that you are using in other recipes, allows the gentle personality that is hidden behind their sharpness to come out." —M.R.

**Serves 4 as a starter or 2 as a main dish**

4 ounces (110g) sliced applewood-smoked bacon

3 large yellow onions (about 12 ounces/340g each)

½ cup (120ml) heavy cream

1 large egg yolk

2 tablespoons unsalted butter

Fine sea salt and freshly ground black pepper

2 tablespoons freshly grated Parmesan cheese, plus extra for sprinkling

1 Stack the slices of bacon, wrap in plastic wrap, and place in the freezer to firm. This will make them easier to cut.

2 To cut the onions using a meat slicer, cut off the root end of each onion and discard. Then cut off the other ends. With a paring knife, core each onion by cutting a cone-shaped piece from the root end of the onion, much as you would remove the stem of an apple. Stand each onion on one end and cut a vertical slit from top to bottom, just reaching the center. This will result in long strands of onion rather than rings when the onion is sliced. Set the slicer to cut ⅛-inch (3mm) slices. Place a flat end of an onion against the blade and slice. Alternatively, to cut by hand (as pictured on pages 116–17), leave the root ends intact, but cut a slit in each onion as above, then cut across the onions to make ⅛-inch (3mm) slices. Separate the onion slices into strands. Place the longer strands in a bowl and reserve the shorter ones for another use. You should have about 8 cups (1.9L) loosely packed onions.

3 Place a steamer basket in a pot over simmering water. Place the onion strands in the basket, cover, and steam for 5 to 10 minutes, until the onions are translucent but still al dente. Taste one to make sure the sharp onion flavor has mellowed to your liking. Remove the basket from the pot. (This can be done a few hours before serving.)

CONTINUED

# Onion Carbonara
## Continued

4 Remove the bacon from the freezer, unwrap, and cut crosswise into ⅛-inch (3mm) strips. Put in a large nonstick skillet and sauté over medium-high heat, stirring often, for about 5 minutes, until crisp and browned.

5 Meanwhile in a small bowl, mix together ¼ cup (60ml) of the cream and the egg yolk. Set aside.

6 Transfer the bacon to paper towels to drain. Pour out the fat and wipe the pan clean with a paper towel. Return the pan to the burner. Add the butter and melt over medium heat. Add the bacon and the remaining ¼ cup (60ml) of cream and simmer for 30 seconds. Add the onions and ½ teaspoon each of salt and pepper. Toss and cook for 2 to 3 minutes, until the onions are hot. Remove the pan from the heat and stir in the reserved cream mixture and the Parmesan. Taste and add additional seasoning, if needed.

7 With a pair of tongs, lift each portion, letting excess sauce drip back into the pan, and arrange in small mounds on the serving plates. Serve sprinkled with additional Parmesan, if desired.

# Sticky Balsamic Ribs

FROM IAN KNAUER

Usually when cooking ribs at home, we're told to take it low and slow. Instead, longtime *Gourmet* editor Ian Knauer will tell you to cook them fast and reckless—425°F (220°C) reckless. Baby backs are more forgiving than bigger spare ribs, and here they get amply marinated and steamed so they come out surprisingly tender, yet sturdy enough to hold up to flipping on the grill. Go too low and slow and you end up with meat falling to pieces and bones sliding out all over the place.

And unlike barbecue recipes that call for a long list of dried spices that come together mysteriously, this one requires only a handful of rather feisty ingredients—and it's clear what each one is doing there. Rosemary and garlic—our friends in so many pork endeavors—are the savory background; cayenne sharpens the garlic's sting; balsamic vinegar and brown sugar bring the sticky, with the sugar leveling out the vinegar's sour.

Serves 8

8 large cloves garlic

4 teaspoons kosher salt (we used Diamond Crystal brand)

2 tablespoons finely chopped rosemary

½ cup (110g) plus 2 tablespoons packed dark brown sugar, divided

1 cup (240ml) plus 2 tablespoons balsamic vinegar, divided

1 teaspoon cayenne pepper

1 teaspoon freshly ground black pepper

8 pounds (3.6kg) baby back pork ribs

1 cup (240ml) water plus 2 cups (475ml) hot water

1 Mince and mash garlic to a paste with 1 teaspoon of the salt. Stir together with the rosemary, 2 tablespoons of the brown sugar, 2 tablespoons of the vinegar, cayenne, remaining 3 teaspoons salt, and pepper. Rub evenly all over the ribs and transfer to 2 large roasting pans in a single layer, meaty side up. Marinate, chilled, for at least

8 hours and up to 24 hours. Alternatively, marinate in a zippered bag or bowl covered with plastic wrap.

2 Preheat the oven to 425°F (220°C) with racks in the upper and lower thirds of the oven.

3 Pour ½ cup (120ml) water into each roasting pan and tightly cover the pans with foil. Roast the ribs, switching the position of the pans halfway through, until the meat is very tender, about 1¾ hours. Remove the pans from the oven and transfer the ribs to a platter.

4 Add 1 cup hot water to each roasting pan and scrape up the brown bits. Skim off and discard the fat, then transfer the liquid to a 10-inch (25cm) skillet. Add the remaining 1 cup (240ml) vinegar and ½ cup (110g) brown sugar and bring to a boil, stirring occasionally. Boil until thick and syrupy and reduced to about 1 cup (240ml), about 15 minutes.

5 In a charcoal grill, prepare a fire for direct-heat cooking over medium-hot charcoal. Alternatively, preheat a gas grill to medium heat. The ribs can also be broiled 3 to 4 inches from heat (instead of grilled) for about 8 minutes.

6 Brush some of the glaze onto both sides of the racks of ribs. Grill, turning occasionally, until the ribs are hot and grill marks appear, about 6 minutes. Brush the ribs with more glaze and serve with the remaining glaze on the side.

# Carnitas

FROM DIANA KENNEDY

Most traditional carnitas recipes call for simmering pork in lard (in Michoacán, this is done in a big copper pot), but I've also seen recipes calling for dry brining, broiling on a rack after an oven braise, deglazing with brandy, simmering in milk, even rigging up a turkey fryer. Without a doubt, all of these methods yield delicious results—there aren't many situations where fatty pork will let you down.

But that's just it: In all of those recipes, the common denominator is fatty pork—which is all you really need. And on those days when you're not up for tracking down several pounds of respectable lard, there is Diana Kennedy's recipe, which is essentially pork + water + salt. This happy threesome simmers away together until the water evaporates and the pork browns in its own rendered fat (a.k.a. *lard*).

Yes, this recipe requires some vigilance once the water has bubbled away and you're left with a shallow pool of burbling fat. You'll need to carefully turn the hunks of pork, and the scent of slow-developing caramelization will be prodding you, belly first, into a state of frenzy. Calm yourself and any hungry-eyed passersby with a cold beer and chips and guacamole (page 45).

Once the pork is tender and crisp in all the right places, you can serve it however you like. The taqueria standard, at least in California, is with minced white onion and cilantro, a variety of salsas, and the occasional hot pickled carrot. Kennedy suggests salsa cruda or guacamole. My favorite way to eat it is bundled into a toasted corn tortilla with shredded cabbage, slivers of ripe avocado, and a shower of lime juice.

**Serves 4 to 6**

3 pounds (1.4kg) good, fatty pork shoulder, butt, or country-style spare ribs, skin and bone removed

Cold water to barely cover

2 teaspoons salt, or to taste

1 Cut the meat, with the fat, into strips about 2 by ¾ inches (5 by 2cm). Barely cover the meat with water in a flameproof pot (the meat will get more evenly cooked if the pot is rather large and shallow), add the salt, and bring it to a boil, uncovered.

2 Lower the flame enough to bring down to a simmer. Let the meat continue simmering until all the liquid has evaporated—about 1½ hours, depending on the shape of your pot. By this time the meat should be cooked through, but not falling apart.

3 Lower the flame a little more and continue cooking the meat until all the fat has rendered out of it. Keep turning the meat until it is lightly browned all over—about 1 hour and 10 minutes.

---

**GENIUS TIP**

As Kennedy points out, you do not want your pork chunks to fall apart. You might think you do, but you don't. So don't cut them too small, or simmer them too vigorously, or otherwise fuss with them too much. If you do, they will stick to the bottom of your pot and eventually disintegrate into scraps of pork confetti.

# Grilled Pork Burgers

## FROM SUZANNE GOIN

Chef Suzanne Goin's perfect burger theory first looks inside the patty itself, instead of just stacking more layers on top. A burger isn't so different from a meatball or crab cake. (You don't just make a ball of meat or a cake of crab—you flavor it!) She starts with ground pork and lards it with minced bacon and fresh Mexican chorizo, as she told me, "To help the meat stay moist, but also to flavor it with all that delicious smoky spiciness." Then, instead of mixing her aromatics and spices straight into the meat, she sautés them together first—sweetening, softening, and unleashing them. With these smart additions, she effectively makes a fresh sausage for the grill.

You could put this on a bun with Manchego and arugula and call it a day. Or you can commit to the full Goin Grilled Pork Burger Experience, which also involves a homemade aïoli and romesco sauce. Both tack on more time, spent dishes, and probably a slow burn in your dominant shoulder area. But all of these components can be made ahead (in fact, the burger mix tastes better made a day in advance), and the aïoli and romesco can be used in other dishes through the week. Best of all, at whatever level you choose to engage with this recipe, the next time you want to make burgers you can take Goin's ideas and riff on them endlessly.

**Makes 6 burgers**

### AÏOLI
1 extra-large egg yolk
½ cup (120ml) grapeseed oil
½ cup (120ml) extra-virgin olive oil
1 small clove garlic
Kosher salt
¼ lemon, for juicing
Pinch of cayenne pepper

### ROMESCO
5 ancho chiles
2 tablespoons raw almonds
2 tablespoons blanched hazelnuts
1¼ cups (300ml) extra-virgin olive oil
1 slice country bread, about 1 inch (2.5cm) thick
⅓ cup (80g) San Marzano canned tomatoes
1 clove garlic, chopped
1 tablespoon chopped fresh flat-leaf parsley
½ lemon, for juicing
Kosher salt

### BURGERS
1½ teaspoons cumin seeds
3 tablespoons extra-virgin olive oil, plus more for grilling
½ cup (80g) diced shallots
1 tablespoon minced garlic
1 tablespoon fresh thyme leaves
2 chiles de arbol, thinly sliced on the bias
1½ teaspoons kosher salt
Freshly ground black pepper
2 pounds (900g) ground pork
4 ounces (115g) fresh Mexican chorizo, casing removed
3 ounces (85g) applewood-smoked bacon, finely diced
2 tablespoons chopped fresh flat-leaf parsley
Olive oil
6 slices Manchego cheese
6 brioche buns or other good burger buns
2 ounces (60g) arugula

**1** **To make the aïoli,** place the yolk in a stainless steel bowl. Begin whisking in the grapeseed oil, drop by drop. Once the mixture has thickened and emulsified, you can whisk in the remaining grapeseed and olive oils in a slow, steady stream. If the mixture gets too thick, add a drop or two of water.

CONTINUED

# Grilled Pork Burgers

## Continued

2 Pound the garlic with ¼ teaspoon salt with a mortar and pestle. Whisk the garlic paste into the aïoli. Season with ¼ teaspoon salt, a squeeze of lemon juice, and the cayenne. Taste for balance and seasoning. If the aïoli seems thick and gloppy, thin it with a little water. In addition to thinning the aïoli, this will also make it creamier. The aïoli will keep, tightly sealed in the refrigerator, for up to 3 days.

3 **To make the romesco,** preheat the oven to 375°F (190°C). Stem and seed the chiles, and then soak them in warm water for 15 minutes to soften. Strain and pat dry with paper towels.

4 Meanwhile, spread the nuts on a baking sheet and toast for 8 to 10 minutes, until they smell nutty and are golden brown.

5 Heat a large sauté pan over high heat for 2 minutes. Add 2 tablespoons of olive oil and wait a minute. Fry the slice of bread on both sides until golden brown. Remove the bread from the pan and cool. Cut it into 1-inch (2.5cm) cubes and set aside.

6 Return the pan to the stove over high heat. Add 2 tablespoons of olive oil and the chiles and sauté for a minute or two. Add the tomatoes. Season with ½ teaspoon salt and cook for 2 to 3 minutes, stirring

often, until the tomato juices have evaporated and the tomato starts to color slightly. Turn off the heat and leave the mixture in the pan.

7 In a food processor, pulse together the toasted nuts, garlic, and fried bread until the bread and nuts are coarsely ground. Add the chile-tomato mixture and process for a minute more. With the machine running, slowly pour in the remaining 1 cup (240ml) olive oil and process until you have a smooth puree. Don't worry, the romesco will "break" or separate into solids and oil; this is normal. Add the parsley and season to taste with lemon juice and more salt, if you like. The romesco will keep, tightly sealed in the refrigerator, for at least a week.

8 **To make the burgers,** in a dry sauté pan, toast the cumin seeds over medium heat for a few minutes, until the seeds release their aroma and darken slightly. Pound the seeds in a mortar or spice grinder until coarsely ground.

9 Return the pan to the stove over high heat for 1 minute. Add the olive oil and shallots. Turn the heat down to medium-low and cook for a few minutes, stirring, once or twice, until the shallots start to soften. Add the garlic, thyme, cumin, and sliced chiles. Season with ¼ teaspoon salt and a few grindings of black pepper, and cook 3 to 4 minutes, until the shallots become translucent. Set aside to cool.

10 In a large bowl, use your hands to combine the ground pork, chorizo, bacon, shallot mixture, and parsley, being careful not to overmix the meat. Season with the remaining 1¼ teaspoons salt and lots of freshly ground black pepper. Shape the meat into six 6-ounce (170g) patties to fit buns. Chill in the refrigerator if not using right away.

11 Light the grill 30 to 40 minutes before cooking and remove the pork burgers from the refrigerator to come to room temperature (if you made them in advance). When the coals are broken down, red, and glowing, brush the pork burgers with olive oil and grill them for 3 to 4 minutes on the first side, until they're nicely browned. Turn the burgers over, and place a piece of cheese on each one. Cook another 3 minutes or so, until the pork is cooked through. (It should still be slightly pink in the center.)

12 Slice the buns in half, brush them with olive oil, and toast them on the grill, cut side down, for a minute or so, until they're lightly browned. Spread both sides of the buns with the aïoli. Place a burger on the bottom half of each bun, and dollop with a generous amount of romesco. Place some arugula leaves on top and finish with the top half of the bun. Serve immediately.

# Brisket of Beef

## FROM NACH WAXMAN

By some accounts, this is the most googled of all brisket recipes. There are unverified reports that it was even served in the White House for the Obamas' first Passover Seder—and for good reason. While other recipes mask brisket with prunes or lemon or dozens of garlic cloves, ketchup or Coca-Cola, this one does nothing of the sort. It has precious few ingredients, applied deliberately and memorably.

Nach Waxman, co-owner of the New York City cookbook store Kitchen Arts & Letters, wove the best parts of two recipes passed down in his family into one simple treatment. From his mother, he learned to avoid adding liquid to the braise and instead to spearhead the seasoning with what he calls a "spectacular quantity of onions" for their subtle, supportive (and moisture-delivering) flavor. From his mother-in-law, he borrowed the trick of slicing the hunk of beef thinly halfway through cooking, then leaning it back on itself like a heap of fallen dominos. At this point, it's fully cooked but still firm, so the slices don't fall to shreds. All the surrounding goodness has more avenues to seep in, making each slice a little like an end piece. (The best part? Discuss.)

Aside from one other delightful step, in which you paint the top of the seared brisket with tomato paste "as if you were icing a cake," that's about it. Then you just cook it, next to one lucky carrot, rather slowly, and for a rather long time.

### Serves 10 to 12

One 16-pound (7.3kg) first-cut (a.k.a. flat-cut) beef brisket, trimmed so that a thin layer of fat remains

1 to 2 teaspoons all-purpose flour (or matzoh meal)

Freshly ground black pepper

3 tablespoons corn oil (or other neutral oil)

8 medium onions, thickly sliced

3 tablespoons tomato paste

Kosher salt

2 to 4 cloves garlic

1 carrot, peeled

1 Preheat the oven to 350°F (175°C).

2 Lightly dust the brisket with flour, then sprinkle with pepper. Heat the oil over medium-high heat in a large ovenproof enameled cast-iron pot or other heavy pot with a lid, just large enough to hold the brisket snugly. Add the brisket to the pot and brown on both sides until crusty brown areas appear on the surface here and there, 5 to 7 minutes per side.

3 Transfer the brisket to a platter, turn up the heat a bit, then add the onions to the pot and stir constantly with a wooden spoon, scraping up any browned bits stuck to the bottom of the pot. Cook until the onions have softened and developed a rich brown color but aren't yet caramelized, 10 to 15 minutes.

4 Turn off the heat and place the brisket and any accumulated juices on top of the onions. Spread the tomato paste over the brisket as if you were icing a cake. Sprinkle with salt and more pepper, then add the garlic and carrot to the pot. Cover the pot, transfer to the oven, and cook the brisket for 1½ hours.

CONTINUED

# Brisket of Beef
## Continued

5 Transfer the brisket to a cutting board and, using a very sharp knife, slice the meat across the grain into approximately ⅛-inch (3mm) thick slices. Return the slices to the pot, overlapping them at an angle so that you can see a bit of the top edge of each slice. The end result should resemble the original unsliced brisket leaning slightly backward. Check the seasonings and, if the sauce appears dry, add 2 to 3 teaspoons of water to the pot.

6 Cover the pot and return to the oven. Lower the heat to 325°F (165°C) and cook the brisket until it is fork-tender, 1½ to 2 hours. Check once or twice during cooking to make sure that the liquid is not bubbling away. If it is, add a few more teaspoons of water—but not more. Also, each time you check, spoon some of the liquid on top of the roast so that it drips down between the slices. It is ready to serve with its juices, but, in fact, it's even better the second day. It also freezes well.

**GENIUS TIP**

To reheat (it's better this way), cool and refrigerate the brisket, onions, and all their cooking juices in the pot you cooked it in. The next day you can scrape away as much of the chilled fat on the surface as you like and pop the brisket into a 200°F (95°C) oven. It should take about an hour to heat through, but there's no harm in starting it early, as long as you check it occasionally to make sure the liquid isn't evaporating away. You can add a little more liquid, if needed, to expand the sauce. I recommend spooning the sticky dregs from the pot over mashed sweet potatoes.

# Meatballs

## FROM RAO'S

Spaghetti and meatballs doesn't have to be a meal that you simmer all day, nor does it need to put you into hibernation once you've eaten it.

Other great meatball recipes rely on milk or even mayonnaise for their tenderness and personality. This one from Rao's restaurant in New York City has the most unexpected secret ingredient of all: lots of tepid water. It's going to look like way too much (2 cups for 2 pounds of meat?). You will also doubt you can serve very many people with this. But that's before you dump your water over the rest of your ingredients, and see the bread crumbs quickly start rehydrating. Like little sponges, they suck up all available liquid, expanding and lightening the mix. Now you have meat, garlic, cheese, and herbs, all delicately clinging together with a little egg and a lot more wet, willing bread.

I've found that you can mix, shape, and fry these meatballs in exactly the time it takes to whip up Marcella Hazan's tomato sauce with onion and butter (page 151). Then you'll plunk them into the sauce for 15 minutes to finish cooking. You could just slip them straight into the sauce to cook instead, but when you fry until they're good and brown first, you're invoking the Maillard reaction—caramelizing all the cobbled surfaces and cranking up the rich, meaty flavor, which it then generously shares with the sauce.

Whether you want to tell your guests that their spaghetti and meatballs took 1 hour, not 10 (and mention the pint of water), that's up to you.

**Makes about 28 meatballs**

1 pound (450g) lean ground beef

8 ounces (225g) ground veal

8 ounces (225g) ground pork

2 large eggs

1 cup (100g) freshly grated Pecorino Romano cheese

1½ tablespoons chopped fresh flat-leaf parsley

½ small clove garlic, minced

Kosher salt or sea salt

Freshly ground black pepper

2 cups (165g) fresh bread crumbs

2 cups (475ml) lukewarm water

1 cup (240ml) good-quality olive oil, for cooking

Your favorite marinara sauce (such as Marcella Hazan's tomato sauce with onion and butter, page 151)

Pasta, for serving (optional)

1 Combine the beef, veal, and pork in a large bowl. Add the eggs, cheese, parsley, and garlic. Season with salt and pepper. Using your hands, blend the ingredients together. Mix the bread crumbs into the meat mixture. Slowly add the water, 1 cup (240ml) at a time, until the mixture is quite moist. (If you want to make sure the seasoning is to your liking, fry off a small test meatball, taste, and adjust.) Shape into 2½- to 3-inch (6.5 to 7.5cm) balls.

2 Heat the oil in a large sauté pan. When the oil is very hot but not smoking, fry the meatballs in batches. When the bottom half of each meatball is very brown and slightly crisp, turn and cook the top half. Remove from the heat and drain on paper towels.

3 Heat the marinara sauce to simmering. Lower the cooked meatballs into the simmering sauce and cook for 15 minutes. Serve alone or with pasta.

---

**GENIUS TIP**

This recipe works best if you make your own fresh bread crumbs (that is, grind or grate some stale bread). In a pinch, if you need to use finer, store-bought bread crumbs, cut back by half, and don't use quite as much water. (The full measure of store-bought crumbs would give you something resembling a stiff, mealy dumpling.)

# Salt-Crusted Beef Tenderloin Grilled in Cloth (Lomo al Trapo)

FROM STEVEN RAICHLEN

This recipe from Steven Raichlen, the author of *The Barbecue! Bible*, has more in common with a crafting project than cooking and will make your dinner guests think you've finally gone too far, until they taste it. Its name translates to "beef tenderloin in cloth" and it goes like this: Cake a big, hunky piece of filet mignon in salt sprinkled with dried oregano, tie it in an old rag, and throw it in flaming coals. Nineteen minutes later you will have dinner.

There isn't much to the tenderloin, as muscles go—it's tender as promised, but lacking the flavor and intrigue of other cuts of beef. We normally serve it in a pool of sauce to make up for that, but here you don't need to—a salt crust and a little temerity liven it up in so many ways.

Naturally, the salt seasons the meat—but not too much. The crust is packed on at the last minute and most of it is brushed away. The thick layer of salt also seals off the surface, allowing the beef to simultaneously roast and steam in its own juices (plus salt and oregano juices). The crust also diffuses the direct heat of the coals, while creating a miniature kiln. In doing so, it gives the beef a texture almost like a sous vide filet. Instead of a bulls-eye leading from a rare center to a charred crust, you get an extended radius of medium-rare, tender all the way to the edge.

This may seem like quite a lot to commit to. Beef tenderloin isn't cheap. A practice run could set you back a good $25 and one dish towel. As much as you want to be a badass pit master, you're probably worried that you will bust open the salt only to find a well-done lump. Good news: You have insurance. You can push an instant-read thermometer through the salt crust to be certain.

**Serves 2**

2 cups (280g) kosher salt (we used Diamond Crystal brand)

1 tablespoon dried oregano

One 12- to 16-ounce (340 to 450g) center-cut beef tenderloin, about 6 inches (15cm) long, meticulously trimmed of all fat and silver skin

Special equipment: 1 piece of clean cotton cloth, approximately 16 inches square (40 by 40cm), dipped in cold water and wrung out slightly; butcher's string

1 Arrange the cotton cloth on a work surface on the diagonal (like a diamond), so that one corner points down toward you. Spread the salt on top of the cloth to form a layer ¼ inch (6mm) thick and extending to within 1 inch (2.5cm) of the edge of the cloth. Sprinkle the oregano evenly over the salt.

2 Arrange the beef tenderloin crosswise on top of the salt about 4 inches (10cm) up from the point of the cloth closest to you; the tenderloin should be parallel to your shoulders. Starting at the corner closest to you, roll the tenderloin up in the cloth and salt. The idea is to make a compact roll. Now take the points of cloth at each end of the resulting cylinder and tie them together on top of the tenderloin. Tuck in any loose ends. The goal is to form a tight cylinder. (If necessary, tie the center of the cylinder with butcher's string to secure it.) You should roll up the tenderloin just prior to grilling.

3 *If you are using a charcoal grill,* light the coals in a chimney starter. When the coals are evenly covered with white ash, rake them out in an even layer at the bottom of the grill. You will not need a grill grate. Place the wrapped tenderloin right on the coals, knotted side up, and grill it for about 9 minutes. Using long-handled tongs, gently turn the tenderloin package over and grill it, uncovered, for about 8 minutes longer. Do not

CONTINUED

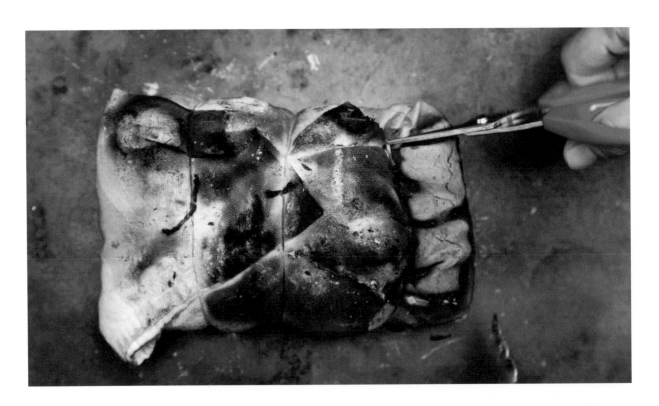

# Salt-Crusted Beef Tenderloin Grilled in Cloth
## Continued

be alarmed if the cloth burns; it's meant to. In fact, the whole package should look about as appetizing as a fire-charred log.

*If you are using a gas grill,* preheat it as hot as it will go. There is no need to oil the grill grate. Place the wrapped tenderloin on the hot grate, knotted side up, and grill it for about 9 minutes. Using long-handled tongs, gently turn the tenderloin package over and grill it for about 8 minutes longer. You may need a little more cooking time and the crust won't burn as black as when charcoal grilled, but the tenderloin will still turn out pretty tasty.

4 Use an instant-read thermometer to test the tenderloin for doneness, inserting it through the cloth and the salt into the center of the meat. When cooked to rare, the internal temperature will be about 125°F (52°C); to medium-rare, 140°F to 145°F (60°C to 63°C).

5 Transfer the charred tenderloin to a metal platter or rimmed sheet pan and let it rest for 2 minutes. Lift the tenderloin with tongs and tap it hard with the back of a large, heavy chef's knife (you may need to tap it several times). The burnt shell should crack and come off. Using a pastry brush, brush any excess salt off the tenderloin. Transfer the tenderloin to a clean platter, cut it into two to four pieces and serve at once.

**GENIUS TIP**

I'm tempted to advise against substituting cheesecloth, the most disposable of kitchen fabrics, because when I tried, the cloth was so flimsy that it burned away in large patches. But the salt crust held and the beef was still perfect. So if you want to spare your towels, you can use cheesecloth—just don't disturb it until the crust has solidified.

"It looks positively prehistoric when it's done (a guaranteed showstopper) and, damn, if it isn't the best way I've found to grill a beef tenderloin." —S.R.

# Perfect Pan-Seared Steaks

## FROM J. KENJI LÓPEZ-ALT

You can cook a better (and more forgiving) steak—but you'll have to toss out all the rules you've learned. Lucky for us, J. Kenji López-Alt of Serious Eats has done the research and can tell us what works and what doesn't. He'll have you salt the steak early, sear it cold, and flip it constantly—and here's why.

Common wisdom is to salt steaks just before cooking, to keep from drawing out their moisture, but López-Alt figured out the ideal timing for salting (at least 40 minutes to a few days ahead), which gives you both more insurance against toughness and better-seasoned steak (see more about how dry-brining works on page 111).

As for taking the steak out of the fridge ahead of time, which many recipes recommend—don't bother. Thick steaks can barely shake off the chill and waiting around for them makes no difference. (And do use steaks at least 1½ inches/4cm thick and portion them out in slices; thinner ones are harder to cook evenly.)

You probably learned to flip steak only once to develop a good, hard sear, but that means you need to know how long each side is going to take, which takes practice (and steak). In this method, you'll flip every 15 seconds or so for a wider-reaching tenderness through the interior, since each side gets a breather to cool down between flips. An instant read thermometer will give you more of a guarantee of perfect doneness, but even if that fails, you have more leeway when flipping frequently. And, as you can see, getting a handsome sear won't be a problem.

**Serves at least 2**

2 bone-in rib-eye, strip, T-bone, or porterhouse steaks, at least 1½ inches (4cm) thick, about 1 pound (450g) each
Kosher salt
Freshly ground black pepper
2 tablespoons neutral oil (such as vegetable or canola)
2 tablespoons butter
A few thyme sprigs and sliced shallots (optional)

1 Pat the steaks dry with paper towels. Season liberally on all sides (including edges) with salt and pepper. Allow to rest uncovered for at least 40 minutes and up to 3 days in the refrigerator on a rack over a rimmed baking sheet. (There is no need to allow the steak to come down to room temperature before cooking.)

2 Heat the oil in a large stainless steel or cast-iron skillet over high heat until heavily smoking. Add steaks to the pan and cook, flipping every 15 to 30 seconds with tongs or a cooking fork, until the internal temperature reaches 110°F (43°C) for rare or 130°F (55°C) for medium (the steak will continue to cook for a bit), 6 to 12 minutes depending on its thickness. Add the butter and aromatics to the pan and continue to cook for an additional 2 minutes, tipping the pan and spooning the sizzling butter over the steak. Remove the steak from the pan and tent it loosely with foil. Allow to rest for at least 5 minutes before serving.

### GENIUS TIP

It's never a bad idea to sear the fatty edge of the steak first, a trick learned from Alain Ducasse. This way, you have rendered steak fat to cook with, not just neutral oil. Your finished steak will also look and taste better, with a crispy brown edge.

# Meatless Mains

# Cauliflower Steaks

## FROM DAN BARBER

If you carve two thick planks from a cauliflower's middle, the cross-sections hold together much better than you'd think—well enough that you can fry them up like a steak. Dan Barber then simmers the remaining florets till soft in water and milk and blitzes them into a weightless white cloud.

You could just make one part of this recipe or the other, but, like a chicken-fried steak surrendering to its cream gravy, there is something deeply appealing about slashing through your slab of cauliflower and plunging it into the downy bed of puree. The cauliflower's sweet, subtle flavors are unobscured; its textures, on both ends of the spectrum, are at their best. Barber brings together the nutty crisped edges you get from roasting and the unearthly richness of a puree (as we learned in Paul Bertolli's cauliflower soup on page 88, whipping up cauliflower's natural pectin turns it creamy without adding any dairy).

How to serve this? The steaks work best at the center of the plate. Add a sturdy kale salad (page 74) or serve the steaks as a first course at a dinner party before herbed salmon (page 97). Or maybe with a nice side of cauliflower (just kidding).

**Serves 2**

One 1½-pound (680g) head cauliflower
1½ cups (360ml) water
1 cup (240ml) whole milk
2 tablespoons vegetable oil, plus more for brushing
Salt and freshly ground black pepper

1 Preheat the oven to 350°F (175°C).

2 Using a sharp, heavy knife and starting at the top center of the cauliflower head, cut two 1-inch (2.5cm) thick slices of cauliflower, cutting through the stem end. Set the cauliflower steaks aside.

3 Cut enough florets from the remaining cauliflower head to measure 3 cups (300g). Combine the florets, water, and milk in a medium saucepan and sprinkle with salt and pepper. Bring to a boil and cook until cauliflower florets are very tender, about 10 minutes. Strain, reserving 1 cup (240ml) of the cooking liquid.

4 Transfer the florets to a blender. Add ½ cup (120ml) of the reserved cooking liquid and puree until smooth. Add more of the liquid, if desired, and puree again. Return the puree to the same saucepan.

5 Heat the 2 tablespoons vegetable oil in heavy, large ovenproof skillet over medium-high heat. Brush the cauliflower steaks with additional oil and sprinkle with salt and pepper. Add the cauliflower steaks to the skillet and cook until golden brown, about 2 minutes per side. Transfer the skillet to the oven and bake the cauliflower steaks until tender, about 10 minutes.

6 Rewarm the cauliflower puree over medium heat. Divide the puree between two plates; top each with cauliflower steak and serve.

# Pasta with Yogurt & Caramelized Onions

## FROM DIANE KOCHILAS

When cookbook author Diane Kochilas began dressing pasta with yogurt, her intention was to adapt a classic Greek island dish that required an obscure cheese called *sitaka*. But, in doing so, she created a dinner of convenience that's striking enough to serve to company. The sauce has only two components: thick yogurt and starchy, salty pasta cooking water, which together create the soothing texture of an alfredo sauce, lightened up with yogurt's tang. But it won't taste austere, especially once you garnish with caramelized onions and Pecorino to balance out the sweetness and salt.

When Kochilas developed this recipe, in order for the yogurt to thicken enough to coat the pasta—and not slip off into a puddle at the bottom of the plate—you had to remember to strain it for 2 hours. This is hardly something to grumble about, but it did keep this dish in the realm of dinners you have to think about before you're hungry.

Now, with the widespread availability of thick, Greek-style (that is, already strained) yogurts, this is an almost embarrassingly ready-to-eat food. The only step that takes time is caramelizing the onions, which you'll want to do right. Give them at least 20 to 30 minutes, while you do everything else. They should look like stained glass when you're done, and taste like honey.

### GENIUS TIP

There are endless ways you can fancy up this meal. Throw in spinach or chard as the pasta finishes boiling. Or blend the sauce with peas, mint, or tahini.

### Serves 4 to 6

5 tablespoons extra-virgin olive oil

6 cups (1.4L) coarsely chopped or sliced onions

Sea salt

1 pound (450g) tagliatelle or other fresh pasta

2 cups (450g) thick, strained Greek-style yogurt (see note below)

1 cup (100g) coarsely grated kefalotyri or Pecorino Romano cheese

1 Heat the olive oil in a large skillet over medium-high heat and add the onions. Decrease the heat to medium-low and cook, stirring frequently and seasoning with salt to taste as you go, until the onions are soft and golden brown, 20 to 30 minutes.

2 Meanwhile, fill a large pot with water and bring to a boil. As the water heats, add enough salt so that you can taste it. Add the pasta and cook until soft, just past al dente. Drain the pasta, reserving ½ cup (120ml) of the pasta water. Combine the yogurt with ¼ cup (60ml) cooking water and mix well. Add more of the reserved pasta water as needed to get the sauce to your desired thickness. Toss the pasta with the yogurt mixture. Serve the pasta immediately, sprinkled generously with cheese and topped with the caramelized onions and their juices.

NOTE: If not using thick, Greek yogurt, line a colander with cheesecloth and set over a bowl or in the sink. Add the yogurt and let drain for 2 hours before proceeding with the recipe. For a treat, seek out sheep's milk yogurt for this.

# Mushroom Bourguignon

## FROM DEB PERELMAN

This version of boeuf bourguignon will do everything a bourguignon needs to do and will do it in time for dinner tonight. There is no beef in it. You won't care.

Deb Perelman, author of the popular blog *Smitten Kitchen* and a former vegetarian who was looking for celebratory meatless mains, designed this recipe based on Julia Child's classic boeuf bourguignon, a favorite dish of her mother's.

There's a fair amount of chopping and slicing up front, but by the time you start cooking, you're nearly done. In only 30 minutes of simmer time, you get a warming and complex stew, thanks to some stand-up red wine, a few aromatics, and umami (mushrooms are loaded with it). To make the sauce richly concentrated, thick, and glossy, you don't need to simmer all day, just swirl in a little butter and flour paste (a.k.a. *beurre manié*) in the last 10 minutes.

In another nontraditional but brilliant move, Perelman serves this with a spoonful of sour cream, a nod to another beefy classic: stroganoff—especially if you serve it over egg noodles, though polenta (page 148) is just as good.

---

### GENIUS TIP

With my medium-size Dutch oven, I like to sear the mushrooms in a few batches so they can sizzle without steaming—this builds up a good layer of toasty residue to deglaze later.

### Serves 4

2 tablespoons olive oil

2 tablespoons butter, softened

2 pounds (900g) portobello or cremini mushrooms, sliced ¼-inch (6mm) thick

1 cup (130g) pearl onions (thawed if frozen)

½ carrot, finely diced

1 small yellow onion, finely diced

1 teaspoon fresh thyme leaves

Salt and freshly ground black pepper

2 cloves garlic, minced

1 cup (240ml) full-bodied red wine

2 tablespoons tomato paste

2 cups (475ml) beef or vegetable broth (beef broth is traditional, but use vegetable to make it vegetarian; the dish works with either)

1½ tablespoons all-purpose flour

Egg noodles, for serving (buttered potatoes or farro or polenta work well, too)

Sour cream and chopped fresh chives or parsley, for garnish (optional)

1 Heat 1 tablespoon of the olive oil and 1 tablespoon of the butter in a large Dutch oven or heavy saucepan over high heat. Sear the mushrooms and pearl onions until they begin to take on a little color, but the mushrooms do not yet release any liquid, 3 to 4 minutes. Remove them from the pan and set aside. Lower the flame to medium and add the second tablespoon of olive oil. Toss the carrot, diced onion, thyme, a few good pinches of salt, and several grinds of black pepper into the pan and cook for 10 minutes, stirring occasionally, until the onions are lightly browned. Add the garlic and cook for just 1 more minute.

CONTINUED

# Mushroom Bourguignon
## Continued

2 Add the wine to the pot, scraping any stuck bits off the bottom, then turn the heat all the way up and reduce it by half. Stir in the tomato paste and the broth. Add back the mushrooms and pearl onions with any juices that have collected and bring to a boil. Then decrease the heat so the mixture simmers for 20 minutes, or until mushrooms are very tender.

3 Thoroughly combine the remaining 1 tablespoon of butter and the flour with a fork; stir it into the stew. Lower the heat and simmer for 10 more minutes. If the sauce is too thin, boil it down to reduce to the right consistency. Season to taste.

4 To serve, spoon the stew over a bowl of egg noodles (or buttered potatoes, farro, or polenta), dollop with sour cream, and sprinkle with chives or parsley.

## Polenta Facile
ADAPTED FROM CARLO MIDDIONE

The polenta you can abandon is also the creamiest polenta—even when you add nothing but water. With this technique, you won't need to stir continuously for 45 minutes. You don't even need to pay very much attention. To serve 8, bring 2 cups (245g) coarse polenta, 1 tablespoon salt, and 2 quarts (1.9L) of water to a boil, stirring occasionally, then set it over slow-simmering water, and cover it. (Use a double boiler if you have one, or just rig up a smaller bowl or pot and cover with foil.) Let it cook for about 1½ hours, stirring every 30 minutes or so. Taste for doneness: The polenta should be very yellow, smooth, shiny, and sweet-tasting. If it is still slightly bitter, cook it longer. Polenta facile can be held in a slowly simmering double boiler in perfect condition for up to 4 hours.

This makes it perfect for a dinner party, or anytime you want to get cooking well before dinner time and go about your business. What's more—the longer it sits, the better it gets. Any bitterness fades; every gritty grain swells and turns creamy. You can make it with stock or add milk or cream or cheese, but even straight water-based polenta will taste better than it has a right to.

# Tomato Sauce with Butter & Onion

## FROM MARCELLA HAZAN

"Simple doesn't mean easy," Marcella Hazan wrote in 2004, a quote widely cited to explain her cooking style and influence. "I can describe simple cooking thus: Cooking that is stripped all the way down to those procedures and those ingredients indispensable in enunciating the sincere flavor intentions of a dish."

In her famous tomato sauce, all you do is simmer tomatoes for 45 minutes with butter and a split onion. The full, true tomato flavor is a revelation, as is finding out you don't need to cook in layers of garlic and herbs to get there (and you're better off without them).

The recipe has found new life online, as bloggers have zeroed in on the fact that Hazan's recipe is well suited to a can of whole, peeled tomatoes. It does make an excellent year-round sauce that way. But fresh tomatoes are really just better—they turn into sauce that tastes like pure summer, to stock your freezer.

Unless you like a sauce with lots of texture, they'll require one extra, rather satisfying step: peeling. See the genius techniques at right for your options. You then simmer away with the swirling butter and bobbing onion, until "the fat floats free from the tomato"—which, of course, you should just stir back in. Then Hazan has you remove the onion, but it's too good not to eat—in the pasta or on its own.

### Serves 6

2 pounds (900g) fresh, ripe tomatoes, prepared as described at right, or 2 cups (480g) canned imported Italian tomatoes, cut up, with their juice

5 tablespoons (70g) butter

1 medium onion, peeled and cut in half

Salt

1 to 1½ pounds (450 to 680g) pasta, cooked, for serving

Freshly grated Parmigiano-Reggiano cheese, for serving

1 Put either the prepared fresh tomatoes or the canned in a saucepan; add the butter, onion, and salt; and cook, uncovered, at a very slow, but steady simmer for about 45 minutes, or until it is thickened to your liking and the fat floats free from the tomato. Stir from time to time, mashing up any large pieces of tomato with the back of a wooden spoon.

2 Taste and correct for salt. Discard the onion before tossing with pasta. Serve with freshly grated Parmigiano-Reggiano cheese for the table.

### GENIUS TECHNIQUES

There are three ways to make fresh tomatoes ready for sauce, all of which use ripe plum tomatoes (or other varieties, if they are equally ripe and truly fruity, not watery).

For *the blanching method*: Plunge the tomatoes in boiling water for a minute or less. Drain them and, as soon as they are cool enough to handle, skin them and cut them into coarse pieces.

*The freezing method* (from David Tanis via *The Kitchn*): Freeze the tomatoes on a baking sheet until hard. Thaw again, either on a rimmed plate on the counter or under running water. Skin them and cut them into coarse pieces.

And lastly, *the food mill method*: Wash the tomatoes in cold water, cut them lengthwise in half, and put them in a covered saucepan. Turn on the heat to medium and cook for 10 minutes. Set a food mill fitted with the disk with the largest holes over a bowl. Transfer the tomatoes with any of their juices to the mill and puree.

# Grilled Pizza

## FROM AL FORNO

To the frustration of home cooks with ambitions of restaurant-caliber pizza, the oven dial maxes out around 500°F (260°C)—not nearly enough to get the best, blistered crust. Proper coal-fired pizza ovens get closer to 900°F (480°C)—how can we hope to match that? *Vogue*'s food critic Jeffrey Steingarten famously documented trying to get around this, risking both his oven and his home.

But there is a better way: If you take to the grill, you inch closer to the proper heat—and a chewy, handsomely charred crust. George Germon and Johanne Killeen at Al Forno restaurant in Providence, Rhode Island, are credited with developing this technique for the single heat source of a hot grill. They soak the dough in oil before patting it flat, to keep it from sticking. Once they set it on the grill, it will only stay there long enough to firm up and show the marks of the grate. Then they flip and top, and serve—all in about 3 minutes. This will take you a bit of practice, but it will be worth it—happily, this recipe makes plenty of dough. (Plan on making a bigger batch than you need the first time; if you have any left over, you can always freeze it.)

This classic margherita variation is as simple as it gets, but Germon and Killeen offer other combinations: bean puree, olive, and tomato; prosciutto, egg, and Parmigiano-Reggiano. Top as you like, but don't overload any one pizza, or you're likely to lose some toppings to the coals.

**Serves 12**

### DOUGH

1 (¼ ounce/7g) envelope active dry yeast

1 cup (240ml) warm water

Pinch of sugar

2¼ teaspoons kosher salt

¼ cup (40g) johnnycake meal or fine-ground white cornmeal

3 tablespoons whole wheat flour

1 tablespoon virgin olive oil

2½ to 3½ cups (310 to 440g) unbleached all-purpose flour

Extra-virgin olive oil

3 cups (300g) freshly grated Parmigiano-Reggiano cheese

1½ cups (150g) freshly grated Pecorino Romano cheese

3 cups (310g) shredded Fontina cheese

4½ cups (1kg) chopped canned tomatoes in heavy puree

¾ cup (45g) chopped fresh flat-leaf parsley

Chiffonade of basil, for garnish (see page 77)

1 **To make the dough,** dissolve the yeast in the warm water with the sugar. After 5 minutes, stir in the salt, johnnycake meal, whole wheat flour, and oil. Gradually add the all-purpose flour, stirring with a wooden spoon until a stiff dough forms. Place the dough on a floured board and knead it for several minutes, adding only enough additional flour to keep the dough from sticking. (Alternately, use olive oil—see Genius Tip on page 154.) When the dough is smooth and shiny, transfer it to a bowl that has been brushed with olive oil. To prevent a skin from forming, brush the top of the dough with additional olive oil, cover the bowl with plastic wrap, and let rise in a warm place, away from drafts, until doubled in bulk, 1½ to 2 hours. Punch

CONTINUED

# Grilled Pizza
## Continued

down the dough and knead once more. Let the dough rise again for about 40 minutes. Punch down the dough. If it is sticky, knead in a bit more flour.

2 Divide the dough into four balls. Cover the balls with plastic wrap and allow to rise at room temperature for about 45 minutes. While the dough is rising, prepare a hot charcoal fire, setting the grill rack 3 to 4 inches (7.5 to 10cm) above the coals and set out topping ingredients.

3 Invert a large baking sheet and brush with 1 to 2 tablespoons extra-virgin olive oil. Place a ball of dough on the oiled surface. Turn the dough over to coat it with oil. With your hands, spread and flatten the pizza dough into a 10- to 12-inch (25 to 30cm) free-form circle, 1/8-inch (3mm) thick—do not make a lip. If you find the dough shrinking back into itself, allow the dough to rest for a few minutes, then continue to spread and flatten the dough. You may end up with a rectangle rather than a circle; the shape is unimportant. Take care not to stretch the dough so thin that small holes appear. If this happens, all is not lost. Rather than trying to repair them, avoid them when adding toppings and drizzling with olive oil.

4 When the fire is hot, use your fingertips to lift the dough gently by the two corners closest to you, and drape it onto the grill. Catch the loose bottom edge on the grill first and guide the remaining dough into place over the fire. Within a minute, the dough will puff slightly, the underside will stiffen, and grill marks will appear.

5 Using tongs, immediately flip the crust over onto the coolest part of the grill. Quickly brush the grilled surface with 2 teaspoons of virgin olive oil. Spread 1/4 cup (25g) Parmigiano-Reggiano cheese, 2 tablespoons Pecorino Romano cheese, 1/4 cup (25g) Fontina cheese over the entire surface of the pizza. Dollop with 6 tablespoons of the tomatoes and top with 1 tablespoon of the parsley. Drizzle the entire pizza with virgin olive oil.

6 After the toppings have been added, slide the pizza back toward the hot coals so about half of the pizza is directly over the heat. Rotate the pizza frequently so that different sections receive high heat, checking the underside by lifting the edge with tongs to be sure it is not burning—if it starts to burn, move to a cooler part of the grill, and cover as needed to heat the top. The pizza is done when the top is bubbling and the cheese has melted. Garnish with basil and serve immediately. Continue stretching the dough balls and grilling pizzas using the above topping ingredients.

---

**GENIUS TIP**

Consider using olive oil instead of flour to keep bread and pizza doughs from sticking to boards and hands, like British baker and cookbook author Dan Lepard. There's no sticking and no risk of overdoing the flour, which can dry out and toughen the dough. (The oil makes your hands soft, too!)

Lightly oil the work surface and your hands, ball up your dough, then press the heel of your hand down through the center and away from you. Gather up the sides like you're curtsying, then give the dough a quarter turn and push through the middle again. Repeat. Think of it as turning the dough inside out over and over, developing lengthening strands of gluten to give the dough structure and chew. (Pictured opposite.)

MEATLESS MAINS
155

# Ginger Fried Rice

## FROM JEAN-GEORGES VONGERICHTEN & MARK BITTMAN

Fried rice is meant to be a hallmark of kitchen efficiency, yet most recipes and tutorials call for day-old rice (the grains are drier and firmer than freshly cooked rice and will absorb flavor without clumping and sogging). And a dinner that requires advanced leftover coordination is a dinner that will rarely—or never—happen in my kitchen.

When Mark Bittman wrote about Jean-Georges Vongerichten's technique for fried rice in the *New York Times* in 2010, he told us to warm the cooked rice, just until heated through, over medium heat—not a searing wok-fry—and new fried rice opportunities opened up. You can get away with using freshly cooked rice, because Vongerichten has you first crisp up ginger and garlic in your oil until they're so bronzed and crackly you'll think they're burnt. You'll fish them out and save them to sprinkle on at the end. This texture is a revelation and takes the pressure off the rice to be perfectly aired out, flaky, and crisp. Those brown bits are all the resistance you need.

Of course, you don't want steamy rice porridge either, but there are some cheats listed at the end of the recipe. You can apply these lazy hacks to any fried rice you want to make right this second, but they're especially suited to this recipe, a marvel of textures and flavors. Here, a little softness is welcome.

### Serves 4

½ cup (120ml) peanut oil (if you're Mark Bittman) or rendered chicken fat (if you're Jean-Georges Vongerichten)

2 tablespoons minced garlic

2 tablespoons minced ginger

Salt

2 cups (180g) rinsed and dried thinly sliced leeks, white and light green parts only

4 cups (630g) cooked rice, preferably jasmine, at room temperature (see note at right)

4 large eggs

2 teaspoons light or toasted sesame oil

4 teaspoons soy sauce

1 In a large skillet, heat ¼ cup (60ml) of the peanut oil over medium heat. Add the garlic and ginger and cook, stirring occasionally, until crisp and brown, 3 to 5 minutes. With a slotted spoon, transfer to paper towels and salt lightly. Alternatively, you can pour the oil into a heatproof bowl through a fine-mesh strainer, then return the flavorful oil to the pan, reserving the ginger and garlic bits.

2 Reduce the heat under the skillet to medium-low and add 2 tablespoons of the peanut oil and the leeks. Cook for about 10 minutes, stirring occasionally, until very tender but not browned. Season lightly with salt.

3 Raise the heat to medium and add the rice. Cook, stirring often, until heated through. Season to taste with salt.

4 In a nonstick skillet over medium heat, fry the eggs in the remaining 2 tablespoons peanut oil, sunny-side-up, until the white is set but yolk is still runny.

5 Divide the rice among four dishes. Top each with an egg and drizzle with ½ teaspoon sesame oil and 1 teaspoon soy sauce. Sprinkle crisped garlic and ginger over everything and serve.

NOTE: Here are some tips if you're cooking the rice fresh, to make sure it isn't too soggy: When the cooking time is done, leave the rice undisturbed in the pot (uncovered) for 5 minutes, then spread the rice on a tray (or two) to dry out. While you prep the rest of the ingredients, put the rice by an open window or a fan, or pop the tray in the fridge or freezer if you have room.

# Spiced Braised Lentils & Tomatoes with Toasted Coconut

FROM MELISSA CLARK

The next time you're looking at the sack of lentils in your pantry, don't just start boiling them while you figure out the more compelling parts of the meal. If you braise them instead, as *New York Times* columnist and cookbook author Melissa Clark does, you won't need to serve anything else. Toast the lentils first in a mélange of seasonings, as you would rice for risotto. Then cook them in a modest amount of flavorful sauce, so that they have no choice but to plump up with the aggressive flavors all around them. And while that goes on in the corner, round up some very important garnishes. Yogurt, cilantro, and salted butter are naturals, but the toasted coconut and mustard seeds will surprise you. You probably never thought to put this many mustard seeds on top of anything, and you'll want to start doing it more.

Most of this happens in one pot, with little more effort than boiling the lentils plain. And the result is so satisfying (so unlike a side of lentils) that you don't have to come up with a chicken to put on top.

Serves 4 to 6

3 tablespoons unsalted butter

1 bunch scallions, white and light green parts, thinly sliced

2 cloves garlic, finely chopped

1 tablespoon good-quality Madras curry powder

1 tablespoon tomato paste

2 cups (385g) green or brown lentils

12 ounces (340g) ripe, juicy tomatoes, chopped (2 medium), or 2 cups canned plum tomatoes, drained (400g) or a 15-ounce (425g) can of diced tomatoes

1¾ teaspoons kosher salt, plus additional to taste

1 cup (85g) dried, unsweetened coconut flakes

1½ tablespoons black or brown mustard seeds

Salty butter, for serving

Plain whole milk yogurt, for serving (optional)

Chopped fresh cilantro, for serving

1 Melt the unsalted butter in a large saucepan over medium-high heat. Add the scallions, garlic, and curry powder. Cook until the mixture is golden and soft, about 4 minutes. Stir in the tomato paste and lentils and cook until slightly caramelized, 1 to 2 minutes. Add the tomatoes and 1¾ teaspoons salt. Add enough water to cover the mixture by ½ inch (1.3cm). Bring the liquid to a boil over high heat; reduce the heat to medium-low and simmer until the lentils are tender, 25 to 40 minutes. If the lentils begin to look dry while cooking, add more water as needed.

2 In a small, dry skillet over medium heat, toast the coconut flakes, mustard seeds, and a large pinch of salt until the coconut is golden, about 3 minutes.

3 To serve, spoon the lentils into individual bowls. Drop about 2 teaspoons salted butter into each dish. Top with yogurt, cilantro, and the coconut mixture. Serve immediately.

## Baked Brown Rice
ADAPTED FROM ALTON BROWN

Cooking rice should be simple and anxiety-free, but it doesn't always work out that way—especially with brown rice, which often turns out sodden or unevenly cooked. This hands-off method, developed by Alton Brown, is now my go-to for perfect, never-gummy brown rice.

Preheat the oven to 375°F (190°C) with a rack in the middle of the oven. Pour 1½ cups (285g) medium- or short-grain brown rice into an 8-inch (20cm) square glass baking dish. Bring 2½ cups (590ml) water, 1 tablespoon unsalted butter, and 1 teaspoon kosher salt to a boil in a covered saucepan. Pour it over the rice, stir, and cover the dish tightly with a lid or heavy-duty aluminum foil. Bake for 1 hour. Uncover and fluff the rice with a fork, and it's ready to serve about 4. Try it with black pepper tofu (page 170).

# Pasta with Let-My-Eggplant-Go-Free! Puree

## FROM FRANCIS LAM

Eggplant can be a mystery. Will it brown handsomely or stick to the pan? Will its flesh relax, or stay stiff and chewy? Will it be sweet, or bitter and gripped with seeds? Is it a boy or a girl? (This last one is a red herring. See the Genius Tip below for what you should really be looking for.)

This doesn't mean we shouldn't cook eggplant. We should. Once we find a few recipes we trust, we can handle its ambiguities. But if you haven't found yours, or you just don't want to deal with it all, do as food writer and editor Francis Lam does: Let your eggplant *go free*. To avoid the texture struggles altogether, Lam harnesses eggplant's affinity for oil and its talent for turning to mush and makes pasta sauce out of it. You get all of the lovely eggplant flavor and silken texture, with none of the stress.

Best of all, it's often 90°F (32°C) outside during peak eggplant season—and unlike recipes that call for roasting, frying, or singeing over an open flame, this is all done stovetop in a reasonable amount of time, over moderate heat, so you—like the eggplant—can go free too.

---

### GENIUS TIP

Don't listen to people who tell you to look for male or female eggplants—botanically speaking, neither exist (eggplant is a sexless fruit). But seek out fresh, not withered, eggplants that are heavy for their size with taut, firm skin—they're much less likely to be seedy and bitter.

### Serves 4 as a main course, 6 as a starter

Salt

1 pound (450g) eggplant, cut into ½-inch (1.3cm) slices

⅓ cup (80ml) extra-virgin olive oil, plus more to finish

3 cloves garlic, lightly smashed (just flatten them, don't take out your aggression on them)

Leaves from 2 sprigs thyme or oregano, chopped

1 cup (240ml) liquid (stock; water; Lam even uses water left over from cooking lentils)

1 pound (450g) long pasta noodles (spaghetti, linguine, whatever floats your boat)

2 tablespoons minced dried tomatoes

6 leaves basil, cut into a chiffonade (see page 77)

Freshly ground black pepper

1 Lightly salt the slices of eggplant, stack them back together, and let it all hang out for about 20 minutes. This will season it and water will drip out, allegedly removing the bitterness, if it's there.

2 Meanwhile, pour the olive oil into a wide, heavy saucepan, add the garlic cloves, and set over low heat. You're just trying to get them friendly with one another, so don't worry if nothing happens for a while.

3 Dry off the eggplant and cut it into chunks. When you start hearing the garlic sizzle a little and can smell it, drop in your eggplant and stir to coat it all with oil. Turn up the heat a little bit to medium-high, add the thyme, and stir. When the eggplant starts to turn translucent and soften, add the liquid and let it come to a boil, then turn it back down to medium-low. Let it bubble for a bit and cover it, leaving a crack for steam to escape. Stir once in a while so the bottom doesn't stick.

4 Meanwhile, bring a large pot of water to a boil, salt it, and cook the pasta to al dente.

CONTINUED

# Pasta with Let-My-Eggplant-Go-Free! Puree
## Continued

5 Meanwhile, check on the eggplant. The liquid should be mostly absorbed or reduced after about 20 minutes. Once it looks mashable, mash it up with a spoon, and adjust the seasoning with salt and pepper to taste. It should be silky smooth and garlicky and eggplanty and humming with oil.

6 Drain the pasta and toss with the eggplant puree. Stir in the tomatoes and basil and gild the lily with some more oil to serve.

---

**GENIUS TIP**

Leftover pastas aren't usually friendly to reheating. This eggplant pasta actually makes a nice cold or room temperature pasta salad the next day (not all do), but it also turns into a mean frittata. Tucking noodles into a panful of eggs, like Viana La Place and Evan Kleiman do in *Cucina Fresca*, means you can take advantage of their seasoning and springy texture, while protecting the pasta from further cooking. From the leftovers of leftovers files, the frittata, in turn, makes an excellent sandwich filling the next day.

# Kale Panini

## FROM ANDREA REUSING

When we think of a sandwich ransacked from the fridge, it's usually eggs, or grilled cheese, or something salumi-based. But with only a little more effort you can get something more restorative out of a desperate kitchen sweep.

Next time, make a hearty vegetarian panini (no panini press needed), like Chapel Hill-based chef Andrea Reusing does, inspired by the sandwiches served by her friend Billy Cotter at his restaurant Toast. This is a clever way to jam a ton of greens into a sandwich and keep them interesting (they're dressed in the most basic of vinaigrettes and flanked by cheese and spicy pickled peppers).

As long as you have random greens, cheese, bread, and jars of pickles (or olives or capers), the recipe here can be used as a template for many fast, sturdy meals—much better ones than you thought you'd get when you wandered over to the fridge.

### Serves 4

#### PICKLED PEPPERS

4 cups (950ml) loosely packed hot, semi-hot, or sweet fresh chile peppers, with seeds

3 tablespoons kosher salt

¼ cup (50g) sugar

4 cups (950ml) distilled white vinegar

#### PANINI

2 big bunches curly kale (about 1 pound/450g total), stemmed, leaves torn into pieces

1½ tablespoons kosher salt, plus more for salting the water

1 tablespoon olive oil, plus more for grilling

1 tablespoon red wine vinegar

8 slices rustic sandwich bread

10 ounces (280g) farmer's cheese or other crumbly fresh cheese such as queso blanco or feta, broken into chunks

Freshly ground black pepper

1 **To make the pickled peppers,** if your chiles are large, cut them into chunks or rounds. If they are small, simply split them in half lengthwise. Put the peppers in one or more jars with tight-fitting lids. In a bowl, dissolve the salt and sugar in the vinegar. Pour this over the peppers, close the jar, and refrigerate for at least 1 day before using. Makes about 2 cups (475ml); extras keep indefinitely.

2 **To make the panini,** working in batches, blanch the kale in boiling salted water for 3 minutes, until tender. Use a slotted spoon to transfer each batch to a colander. When all the kale is cooked, let it cool and then squeeze with your hands to remove the excess moisture. Cut the kale into ½-inch (1.3cm) wide strips and put them in a bowl.

3 Preheat a panini press if you have one, or heat a large cast-iron skillet over low heat and have another pan of the same size ready to weigh down the sandwiches.

4 Right before you are ready to assemble the sandwiches, season the kale with salt. Add the oil and toss well. Finish with the vinegar. Lay out four slices of bread and top them with equal parts kale and cheese; add chiles to taste. Season with salt and pepper and top with the other slices of bread.

5 Lightly oil the panini press and follow the manufacturer's instructions for grilling the sandwiches. If you are using a pan on the stovetop, raise the heat to medium, lightly oil the pan, and add as many sandwiches as can comfortably fit. Place the other heavy pan on top to press the sandwiches; if the pan is relatively light, add some weight to it, such as a large can or a full tea kettle. Rotating the pan on the burner frequently, cook the sandwiches for about 5 minutes, until deep golden brown. Transfer the sandwiches to a plate, re-oil the pan, and return the sandwiches to the pan, browned side up, to cook the other side, about 3 minutes. Serve immediately.

# Ship's Biscuit

## FROM SALTIE

You might not think there'd be ways to improve upon the egg sandwich—fry an egg, melt some cheese on toast, maybe get a little bacon involved. Crushed together with the yolk as condiment, this is breakfast, sure, but it's also lunch, dinner, or a midnight snack. And for many of us, this happens a lot, so a new egg sandwich is a boon. This one, from Brooklyn sandwich shop Saltie, takes a novel egg-cooking technique— a hybrid of fried and scrambled—and adds very little.

The soft scrambled eggs are really clotted whites, suspended in a barely thickened yolk—something like if you were to slash an over-easy egg to bits. They're served on a piece of split focaccia with ricotta, which acts as both a subtle variation in curdy texture and insulation for the bottom layer of bread. Eating it is a messy operation—but it doesn't last long.

**Makes 1 sandwich**

1 sandwich-size piece of focaccia
About 2 tablespoons fresh ricotta
1 teaspoon unsalted butter
2 large eggs
Sea salt

1 Cut the focaccia in half horizontally and put the bottom half on a plate, cut side up. Spread the ricotta in an even and generous layer on the cut side. Set aside.

2 To soft scramble the eggs, melt the butter in a nonstick skillet over medium heat. Break the eggs into the pan when it is warm but not yet hot. Sprinkle the eggs lightly with salt.

3 Let the pan heat up, and don't move the eggs until the whites begin to set. Using a rubber spatula, move the whites around the pan to help cook through, while keeping the yolk unbroken. When the whites fluff up and are almost completely set, remove from the heat and fold the yolks into the white. The residual heat should cook the whites through and leave the yolks soft. This is kind of like scrambling an over-easy egg. To emphasize: Be careful not to overcook the eggs. Err on the side of runny rather than dry.

4 Spoon the eggs on top of the ricotta. Replace the top of the bread and serve right away.

---

## Grilled Cheese Sandwiches
### ADAPTED FROM GABRIELLE HAMILTON

The secret to crispier, faster, better grilled cheese sandwiches is in slathering the outsides of the bread not with butter, but mayonnaise, like Gabrielle Hamilton, author and chef-owner of Prune. Mayo is slower to burn, which—just like that—solves the biggest challenge of grilled cheese: how to get the insides to heat through before the outside blackens. The oil and egg in mayonnaise also brown and crisp more evenly than butter, creating a glossy crunch from edge to edge.

If you're making a lot of sandwiches, heat the oven to 300°F (150°C). Make as many sandwiches as you like, smearing mayonnaise (Hamilton uses Hellmann's) generously on one side of ½-inch (1.3cm) thick slices of rustic bread. Form sandwiches, mayo-side out, the middles stuffed with shredded extra-sharp cheddar cheese. Heat a large, preferably nonstick frying pan or griddle over medium-low heat until hot, about 4 to 5 minutes. Place 2 to 3 of the sandwiches in the pan and cook until the bottoms are golden brown and the cheese is starting to melt, about 5 minutes. Flip the sandwiches and cook until the second sides are golden brown and the cheese is completely melted, about 5 minutes more. If you need to hold the sandwiches or make more, transfer them to a baking sheet and place them in the oven to keep warm. Let them cool a minute to two before cutting each sandwich in half. Serve with spicy tomato soup (page 87).

# Green Lentil Salad

## FROM PATRICIA WELLS

At a glance, nothing seems special about this recipe. You've probably simmered lentils with aromatics before, and even tossed them in vinaigrette. The genius lies in this recipe's simplicity and cookbook author Patricia Wells's perfect, restrained proportions. When you taste the lentils just after mixing, you might find them bland and watery. But don't give up on them! Let the vinaigrette seep in for 10 minutes. Salt them judiciously, sample, salt some more. All of a sudden, the lentils will taste alive: The cloves, bay, onion and garlic, vinegar, and oil are all there, fragrant and substantive, waiting for you to notice them.

I make these lentils a lot to have on hand through the week. They're best served warm or at room temperature—a perfect lunch to take to work, a friend to all vegetables, a partner for all grains, a bed for all meats. And they're a jumping off point for all kinds of new dishes. A high note: warming them in cream with bacon-braised fennel.

**Serves 8**

1 pound (450g) French green or brown lentils

1 onion, halved and stuck with 2 cloves

1 clove garlic, peeled

1 bay leaf

¼ cup (60ml) red wine vinegar

2 tablespoons extra-virgin olive oil

Salt and freshly ground black pepper

1 Rinse the lentils and discard any pebbles. Place the lentils, onion, garlic, and bay leaf in a saucepan and cover with cold water by 1 inch (2.5cm). Cover and bring to a boil over medium heat. Reduce heat to low and simmer, covered, until lentils are tender, 25 to 35 minutes. Add liquid as needed.

2 Discard the onion, garlic, and bay leaf and drain any excess liquid. Whisk the vinegar, oil, and salt together in a small bowl. Pour over the warm lentils and toss.

3 Before serving, season with pepper and additional salt, if necessary. Serve warm or at room temperature.

# Black Pepper Tofu

## FROM YOTAM OTTOLENGHI

Tofu's proponents have tried to get us to see all the ways to improve its texture—freezing or pressing or boiling to rid it of spare water, broiling or roasting to crisp it up. These are all effective at making tofu friendlier to cook with, but nothing is as guaranteed to seduce a skeptic as dredging tofu in cornstarch and pan-frying it to a shiny crisp, while the inner bits go soft and custardy.

The just-fried nubs are almost too crunchy to eat, which is why it's a good idea to add them to a pan of shallots, chiles, ginger, and garlic that have stewed in butter and soy and heaps of black pepper. In the sauce, the fried cubes will relax just enough, but maintain all the integrity you've fried into them.

This—with some brown rice (page 159)—is as impressive a vegetarian dinner party main dish as you can get. And cheap, too—despite the 11 tablespoons of butter and 5 tablespoons of black pepper. The tofu called for, even organic, costs less than $6 and feeds at least four, generously.

**Serves 4**

Vegetable oil, for frying

1¾ pounds (800g) firm tofu

Cornstarch, to dust

11 tablespoons (150g) unsalted butter

12 small shallots (12 ounces/340g), thinly sliced

8 fresh red chiles (fairly mild ones), thinly sliced

12 cloves garlic, crushed

3 tablespoons finely chopped fresh ginger

3 tablespoons sweet soy sauce (kecap manis)

3 tablespoons light soy sauce

4 teaspoons dark soy sauce

2 tablespoons sugar

5 tablespoons coarsely crushed black peppercorns (use a mortar and pestle or a spice grinder)

16 small, thin green onions, cut into 1¼-inch (3cm) segments

1 Start with the tofu. Pour enough oil into a large frying pan or wok to come ¼ inch (6mm) up the sides and heat over medium-high. Cut the tofu into large cubes, about 1 inch (2.5cm) square. Toss them in some cornstarch and shake off the excess, then add to the hot oil. (You'll need to fry the tofu pieces in a few batches so they don't stew in the pan.) Fry, turning them around as you go, until they are golden all over and have a thin crust. As they are cooked, transfer them onto paper towels.

2 Remove the oil and any sediment from the pan, then add the butter and melt it over low to medium heat. Add the shallots, chiles, garlic, and ginger. Sauté for about 15 minutes, stirring occasionally, until the ingredients have turned shiny and are totally soft. Next, add the soy sauces and sugar and stir, then add the crushed black pepper.

3 Add the tofu to warm it up in the sauce for about a minute. Finally, stir in the green onions. Serve hot.

---

**GENIUS TIP**

Yes, you can ease back on the butter a little. And you can use whatever kind of soy sauce you have, if you adjust the saltiness to taste (and the sweetness, if you need to make up for not having kecap manis, a.k.a. sweet soy).

# Vegetables

# Whole Roasted Cauliflower with Whipped Goat Cheese

## FROM ALON SHAYA

Cauliflower takes well to roasting: All those starchy crevices get nutty and sweet and come into their own—catching oils, crisping, browning, basking. But here's a twist: You don't even need to cut it into florets first. Like a chicken, a cauliflower is roastable by nature.

It's not quite as simple as chucking it in the oven as-is. If you poach your cauliflower in a winey, punchy broth first, as chef Alon Shaya does, you can control the seasoning all the way to the core. At Shaya's New Orleans restaurant, Domenica, this means cooking sous vide, then in an 800°F (425°C) pizza oven. At home, it's a big pot and whatever oven came in your wall.

You might think the thing would have a hard time browning after such a thorough soak, but the small amounts of olive oil and butter in the poaching liquid cling to all the cauliflower's folds and curves, which don't hesitate to brown and crackle up in a hot oven.

While the cauliflower is simmering or roasting away (or even the day before), you can whip up the labneh-like sauce. When you're ready to serve, all that's left is to tip over some olive oil and salt, and carve the cauliflower into wedges or break it off limb by limb.

### Serves 4 to 6

**WHIPPED GOAT CHEESE**

4 ounces (115g) fresh goat cheese

3 ounces (85g) cream cheese

3 ounces (85g) feta cheese

⅓ cup (80ml) heavy cream

2 tablespoons olive oil, plus more for serving

Sea salt

**ROASTED CAULIFLOWER**

2½ cups (590ml) dry white wine

⅓ cup (80ml) olive oil, plus more for serving

¼ cup (35g) kosher salt

3 tablespoons fresh lemon juice

2 tablespoons unsalted butter

1 tablespoon crushed red pepper flakes, or to taste

1 tablespoon sugar

1 bay leaf

1 whole head cauliflower, stem trimmed and leaves removed

Coarse sea salt, for serving

1 **To make the whipped goat cheese,** blend the goat cheese, cream cheese, feta, cream, and 2 tablespoons olive oil in a food processor until smooth; season with sea salt. Transfer the whipped goat cheese to a serving bowl and drizzle with olive oil. The whipped goat cheese can be made 1 day ahead. Cover and chill in the refrigerator.

2 **To make the cauliflower,** preheat the oven to 475°F (245°C).

3 Bring the wine, oil, salt, lemon juice, butter, red pepper flakes, sugar, bay leaf, and 8 cups (1.9L) water to a boil in a large pot. Carefully lower in the cauliflower, reduce the heat, and simmer, turning occasionally, until a knife easily inserts into center, 15 to 20 minutes. Using two slotted spoons or a mesh strainer or spider, transfer the cauliflower to a rimmed baking sheet or roasting pan, draining well.

4 Roast, rotating the pan halfway through, until the cauliflower is brown all over, 30 to 40 minutes.

5 Transfer the cauliflower to a plate. Drizzle with oil; sprinkle with salt. Serve with the whipped goat cheese.

---

**GENIUS TIP**

Save that broth! It can be considered a boozy first course (the vegetarian version of pot-au-feu), or the base for tomorrow's risotto or pasta sauce, or a poaching liquid for cooking more vegetables or fish.

# Broccoli Cooked Forever

## FROM ROY FINAMORE

Broccoli overcooked carelessly tastes stale and murky. But when you push beyond that disappointing just-too-done state (and throw in a whole lot of olive oil bubbling lazily with garlic, anchovy, and hot peppers), you find yourself with a miraculous substance.

Here's what "forever" really means: After blanching your trimmed stems and florets, slip them into an olive oil bath and leave them be, covered, for 2 whole hours. "The blanching is to send the broccoli on its way to foreverland, softening it just a bit so it starts absorbing the flavors in the oil," editor and cookbook author Roy Finamore explained to me. "It also ensures that the broccoli doesn't fry and get crisp at the beginning, when the oil is at its hottest."

I want to call the result broccoli butter, but it's more appropriately broccoli confit. The florets trap all the oil's richness, and the stems melt away. It would be equally at home spooned up onto some sturdy bread, blanketing a good ridged pasta, or layered onto a pizza.

---

### GENIUS TIP

Merrill Stubbs uses the same technique to cook other vegetables forever, like carrots and parsnips—popular with both adults and babies just learning to eat real food. She also uses this recipe as the base for an excellent pureed soup by adding a quart of chicken stock (page 92) at the end of the recipe, simmering for 5 minutes, then blending half of the soup and seasoning to taste with lemon juice and grated Parmesan.

### Serves 4 to 6

2 bunches (2 to 2¼ pounds/900g to 1kg) broccoli

1 cup (240ml) olive oil

3 cloves garlic, sliced thin

2 small hot chiles, halved lengthwise (Finamore likes small fresh red peppers, but you can substitute green Thai chiles, various dried ones, even a big pinch of red chile flakes)

4 anchovy fillets, chopped

Coarse salt and freshly ground black pepper

1  Bring a large pot of water to a boil. While the water is heating, cut the florets off the broccoli. Peel the stems and cut them into rather thick slices, about ⅓ inch (8mm). When the water comes to a boil, add the broccoli and cover the pot to bring it back to a boil quickly. Blanch the broccoli for 5 minutes. Drain.

2  Put olive oil and garlic into a large skillet over medium heat. When the garlic starts to sizzle, add the hot peppers and anchovies. Cook, giving a stir or two, until the anchovies melt. Add the broccoli, season with salt and pepper, and stir well. Cover the skillet, turn the heat to very low, and cook for 2 hours. Use a spatula to turn the broccoli over in the skillet a few times, but try not to break it up. It will be very tender when done.

3  Use a slotted spoon to transfer the broccoli to a serving dish. It is delicious hot or at room temperature.

# Garlic Green Beans

FROM PENELOPE CASAS

In their natural state, green beans can be severe and squeaky. Our goal is to break through that, but we're going about it all wrong.

We tend to blanch beans first thing, even if we're going to sauté them. (I'm not sure why we do that, other than impatience, or an abstract desire for brighter color.) And even if we skipped blanching, we'd probably absently sauté some shallot or garlic, then add the beans—so they end up tasting like sautéed shallot or garlic. None of this leads to bad green beans. But they could be even better.

All you need to do, as I learned from Spanish cookbook author Penelope Casas, is sear the beans in butter, covered, so they stew in their own juices. Then, once they're looking a little saggy and soft, stir in salt and pulverized garlic off the heat. You could use less garlic or leave it out, but its pushy sting will soften a little on the warmth of the beans and frame our focus. Which, of course, is those green beans, sweet and singed and alive, with none of their goodness overwritten or left behind.

**Serves 4**

12 ounces (340g) fresh green beans
1 tablespoon butter
1 clove garlic, crushed
Coarse salt

1 Snap off the tops of the beans. Melt the butter in a skillet over medium heat. Add the beans, and cook them over a medium flame, stirring, until they begin to brown. Lower the flame, cover, and cook for about 20 minutes, until the beans are the desired tenderness, stirring occasionally. Mix in the garlic, sprinkle with salt, and serve immediately.

## Ginger Juice
ADAPTED FROM MOLLY STEVENS

This is another simple, lively way to dress up green beans (or other sautéed or roasted vegetables, or stir-fries, even juices or cocktails). Grate and squeeze fresh ginger to wick out the spicy juice—no peeling, no mincing.

To get about a tablespoon of ginger juice, finely grate a 1½-inch (4cm) piece fresh ginger (about 2 ounces/60g) on a Microplane grater. You should have about 2 tablespoons grated ginger. Squeeze the ginger in a small fine-mesh strainer set over a bowl, extracting as much liquid as possible. Discard the grated ginger and use the juice as you like. Alternatively, you can reuse the grated ginger, though it will lack pungency—or simmer it in water, then strain, to make ginger tea (good with lemon and honey). Both the juice and the grated ginger are best used immediately.

# Balsamic Glazed Beets & Greens

## FROM PETER BERLEY

I'm afraid we don't understand beets as well as we could. We don't get to interact with them when they're roasting in a packet of foil or boiling for an hour in a pot of dark red water.

This recipe from chef and cooking instructor Peter Berley allows us to cook beets faster, like all the other vegetables we know better. We get to cut them bite-size, cook them in a pan on the stovetop, and peek at them anytime we want.

First they braise in water with red onion, balsamic vinegar, butter, and tarragon until tender, then the lid comes off and the liquids reduce down to a syrup. Then, as Berley writes, "The greens are placed on top of the roots, the manner in which they grew." They steam and wilt, then get stirred through the glaze.

Yes, we get to use the whole beet in one pan—including the greens and even the peel—so there's no hanging onto the tops with some unidentified goal, only to forget and throw them away a week later. This is a recipe of efficiency, but you wouldn't know it from how nicely it cleans up on the plate.

Serves 4

1 medium red onion, cut into ¼-inch (6mm) crescents

4 to 5 fresh beets with tops, roots scrubbed, trimmed, and cut into 4 to 6 wedges, greens chopped

3 tablespoons balsamic vinegar

2 tablespoons unsalted butter or extra-virgin olive oil

2 sprigs fresh tarragon, leaves finely chopped

Coarse sea salt and freshly ground black pepper

1 In a heavy pan wide enough to hold the vegetables in a snug single layer, combine the onion, beet roots, vinegar, butter, tarragon, and ½ teaspoon salt. Pour in enough water to barely cover the vegetables and bring to a boil over high heat. Reduce the heat to low and simmer, covered, for 25 minutes, or until the beets are nearly, but not quite, tender.

2 Raise the heat and boil, uncovered, until the liquid has reduced to a syrup and the beets are fork-tender.

3 Add the beet greens, reduce heat, and simmer, covered, for 5 minutes.

4 Uncover and turn the greens over so they mix with the roots and onions. Add pepper and additional salt to taste. Simmer for 2 minutes more and serve.

# Grilled Chard Stems with Anchovy Vinaigrette

### FROM ANNA KLINGER

It's easy to forget that Swiss chard's stems have the same flavor as the leaves, lacking only their gloss and buoyant texture. Instead, the stems can be stringy and prone to fraying at their bottoms. No wonder so many people quietly toss them at the compost bin.

The most resourceful among us have figured out how to chop the stems finely and sauté them with onions and garlic before adding the chopped leaves to the pan: a little whole beast cookery to take pride in. We may also choose to pickle, braise, or gratinée them. But I think Anna Klinger, at Al Di La trattoria, faced with mountains leftover from her signature Swiss chard malfatti, might have devised the most impressive way to tease out the stems' innate sweetness. She blanches them in well-salted water, grills them slowly, then swaddles them in an anchovy vinaigrette.

Give an outcast vegetable scrap a little salty char and a rich, meaty dressing, and you have yourself a side dish. That's an easy takeaway here. But it's also the light hand Klinger uses that makes this recipe more than just that. For the dressing, she soaks salt-packed anchovy fillets in a few changes of milk to mellow out the salt. (Despite what you might be thinking, anchovy milk actually tastes pretty good. Put that stuff in a béchamel!)

This recipe makes more dressing than you'll need, but it keeps. Put it on everything: Your lettuce cores, your carrot tops—what other gems might you be throwing away?

**Serves 4**

### ANCHOVY VINAIGRETTE BASE

2 ounces (60g) anchovies (preferably salt-packed, cleaned, rinsed, and soaked in a few changes of milk; see first step at right)

3 small cloves garlic (½ ounce/15g), minced

¾ cup plus 4 teaspoons (200ml) extra-virgin olive oil

½ teaspoon crushed red pepper flakes, or more to taste

### GRILLED SWISS CHARD STEMS

Stems from 1 large bunch Swiss chard (save the greens for another use, like the herb jam on page 46)

Extra-virgin olive oil

Salt and freshly ground black pepper

Splash of sherry vinegar

1 If you choose to soak the anchovies in milk, cover the fillets in milk by about an inch and soak for 12 to 24 hours, changing the milk once or twice. Taste them periodically for saltiness. They're ready when they have the level of saltiness you like. If oversoaked, they could end up very bland.

2 **To make the vinaigrette base,** blend the anchovies, garlic, olive oil, and red pepper flakes in a blender or food processor until well combined but still a little chunky. This makes a large quantity. It keeps well for at least a week and tastes good on everything.

3 Prepare a charcoal or gas grill for low heat.

4 **To prepare the chard,** wash the chard stems, cut off any dark edges, and cut into 5- to 6-inch (13 to 15cm) lengths. Blanch the stems in salted boiling water in batches until just tender, about 2 minutes per batch, then transfer to an ice bath. It is very important to follow all the rules of blanching and not overcrowd the pot. Any shortcuts here will result in the color of the stems turning black.

5 Dry the blanched stems, toss them lightly with olive oil, salt, and pepper, and place them on the grill in a single layer. Grill long and slow over a low fire until they become quite dark and charred but not burned.

6 Remove the stems from the grill and toss with the anchovy vinaigrette base and a splash of sherry vinegar. Serve warm.

# Roasted Brussels Sprouts with Fish Sauce Vinaigrette

## FROM MOMOFUKU

Even if we've started to recover from mushy brussels sprout flashbacks, we can still take them further than roasting them plain—by shoving them into a puddle of fish sauce vinaigrette, for example.

While fish sauce is nothing you should eat—or, yes, smell—by itself, like an undercurrent of anchovy or soy sauce, it can light up a dressing. Especially when combined with flickers of garlic and chile, bursts of lime and rice vinegar, and cilantro stems, which have all the fragrance of the leaves but more crunch.

You cook the sprouts till they're crackly, with pretty brown surfaces and lots of crevices for the vinaigrette to seep in and bounce around. Momofuku founder and chef David Chang likes to get this going with the sprouts laid face-down in a skillet of sizzling oil before finishing them in the oven.

The original recipe includes some other fun doodads—fried cilantro leaves and spicy toasted puffed rice. I skip them—with a bowl of handsomely roasted sprouts, that vinaigrette, and a finishing blanket of fresh mint and cilantro, any more excitement just wouldn't be fair to the rest of dinner.

Serves 4 to 6

### FISH SAUCE VINAIGRETTE

½ cup (120ml) fish sauce (adjust to taste; some fish sauce brands are saltier than others)

¼ cup (60ml) water, plus more as needed

2 tablespoons rice wine vinegar

Juice of 1 lime, plus more as needed

¼ cup (50g) sugar

1 clove garlic, minced

1 to 3 red bird's-eye chiles, thinly sliced, seeds intact

2 tablespoons very thinly sliced cilantro stems, plus ½ cup (8g) leaves

3 tablespoons chopped fresh mint

2 pounds (900g) brussels sprouts (smaller ones are better)

Grapeseed or other neutral oil (lots for frying, little for roasting)

1 **To make the vinaigrette,** combine the fish sauce, water, vinegar, lime juice, sugar, garlic, and chiles in a jar. Taste; if it is too salty, add more water and/or lime juice. This vinaigrette will keep for up to a week in the refrigerator.

2 Combine the vinaigrette, cilantro stems, and mint in a bowl, and set aside.

3 Peel away any loose or discolored outer leaves from the brussels sprouts, trim the dry ends of the stems with a knife, and cut the sprouts in half. Cut any especially large ones in quarters. Do not wash, especially if frying the sprouts. If roasting, and you must, dry very well.

4 *To roast the brussels sprouts (recommended),* preheat the oven to 400°F (200°C). Heat 2 tablespoons grapeseed oil (or just enough to evenly coat the bottom of the pans) in each of two large oven-safe skillets (12 to 14 inches/30 to 35cm) over medium heat. When the oil slides easily from side to side in the pan, add the brussels sprouts cut side down. When the cut faces of the sprouts begin to

brown, transfer the pan to the oven to finish cooking, about 15 minutes. Alternatively, if you don't have two large skillets or are cooking more sprouts for a larger crowd, roast them in the oven: Toss them with 1 tablespoon of oil per pound and spread them on a baking sheet, cut sides down. Roast in the oven, checking for browning every 10 to 15 minutes, tossing them around with a spatula only once they start to brown nicely. The sprouts are ready when they are tender but not soft, with nice, dark brown color.

*To fry the brussels sprouts*, heat 1½ inches (4cm) of oil in a deep saucepan over medium-high heat until a deep-fry or instant-read thermometer registers 375°F (190°C).

Line a plate or tray with paper towels. Fry in batches that don't crowd the pan—be careful, these will pop and spatter. Brussels sprouts will take about 5 minutes: when the outer leaves begin to hint at going black around the edges—that is, after the sprouts have sizzled, shrunk, popped, and browned but before they burn—remove them to the paper towel-lined plate.

5 Serve warm or at room temperature. When you are ready to serve, divide the brussels sprouts among four bowls (or serve it all out of one big bowl), top with the dressing to taste and cilantro leaves, and toss once or twice to coat.

# Fried Asparagus with Miso Dressing

## FROM NOBU MATSUHISA

Next time you start taking asparagus for granted, make like Nobu Matsuhisa and fry it. (And not in the state-fair, we-can-fry-anything way, or even like tempura. There's no batter to get in the way here.) By taking away the coating, which would crisp but leave the asparagus to steam underneath, you expose the surfaces of the stalks themselves to the slap of hot oil. The skin ripples and shines like that of a striped bass. The tips frizzle, each little purple talon spreads and crisps up all around the edges. The stalks turn vivid green and tender in just a minute or two under the oil. (And you don't need much oil at all—just a couple of inches in a pot wide enough to fit your spears.)

Here's the kicker: Asparagus loves oil. "Because the chemical that makes asparagus taste like asparagus is water-soluble," Thomas Keller writes in *Ad Hoc at Home*, "we gravitate toward other ways to cook them besides blanching them in water, which diminishes some of their flavor." That asparagus-flavor chemical isn't soluble in oil, however, so its sweetness and grassy flavor aren't sapped in an oily bath, but concentrated.

Serves 2 to 4

### MISO DRESSING

3 ounces (90g) white miso or red grain miso (akatsubu miso)

A dab of garlic paste, or 1 small clove garlic, grated

1 teaspoon soy sauce

½ cup (120ml) grapeseed oil

¼ cup plus 2 tablespoons (90ml) rice vinegar

A little sugar syrup, made with equal parts water and sugar (optional)

3 inches (about 7.5cm) white part of 1 leek

Oil, for deep-frying (grapeseed, peanut, or even olive oil)

9 (or more) large spears green asparagus, about 9 ounces (270g)

1 **To make the dressing,** combine the miso with the garlic, soy sauce, grapeseed oil, and vinegar. Check the taste and add the sugar syrup, if desired.

2 Slash the leek lengthwise to open and discard the inner core. Wash off the sand between the layers under running cold water. Cut into thin shreds. Pat dry well.

3 Pour 2 inches (5cm) of oil into a pot wide enough to hold the asparagus. Heat the oil for deep-frying to about 300°F (150°C). Deep-fry the leek until it begins to brown. Scoop the fried leek out with a slotted spoon or spider and drain on a wire rack in warm spot in the kitchen for up to 1 to 2 hours.

4 Reheat the oil up to 320°F to 340°F (160°C to 170°C). Trim off the hard bottom of each asparagus and deep-fry in the oil for 1 to 2 minutes, until the asparagus is bright green and just tender.

5 To serve, cut each length in half crosswise or leave them whole. Spoon the miso dressing on a plate and stack the asparagus on it. Top with the fried leek. Serve immediately.

# Ratatouille

## FROM ALICE WATERS

One school of ratatouille is Julia Child's. In her highly evolved version, every vegetable must be meticulously cut and cooked separately before they "partake of a brief communal simmer," as she described it. She took these pains to ensure that every vegetable maintained its dignity, without melting into a muddy soup, as they do in the other school of ratatouille—whose exponents just dump everything in the pot at once.

Leave it to Alice Waters, longtime champion of vegetable TLC, to show us there is a happy compromise. Her recipe only fusses where it needs to fuss—over the eggplant, which does benefit from a salting and brief time-out to draw out its moisture and bitterness. After patting dry and browning it on its own, the eggplant behaves, turning sweet and bronzed with creamy flesh.

For the rest, Waters simply adds the vegetables to the pot one by one to build flavor, but because they're cut small (½ inch/1.3cm), they don't cook for long and don't have a chance to inherit each other's idiosyncrasies.

Basil is delivered in two stages, via a bouquet that swishes along in the pot the whole time, and a smattering of fresh chopped leaves at the end. A pinch of red chile flakes sharpens the focus, and a finishing swirl of fresh olive oil pulls the sauce together. What you end up with is a humble stew, yes, but one that has every bit of integrity the summer harvest deserves. Eat it hot with fried eggs or spoon it up cold onto torn hunks of bread.

**Serves 6 to 8**

1 medium or 2 small eggplant, cut into ½-inch (1.3cm) dice

Salt

4 tablespoons olive oil, plus more to taste

2 onions, cut into ½-inch (1.3cm) dice

4 to 6 cloves garlic, chopped

½ bunch basil, tied in a bouquet with kitchen twine, plus 6 basil leaves, chopped

Pinch of crushed red chile flakes

2 sweet peppers, cut into ½-inch (1.3cm) dice

3 medium summer squash, cut into ½-inch (1.3cm) dice

3 ripe medium tomatoes, cut into ½-inch (1.3cm) dice

1 Toss the eggplant cubes with a teaspoon or so of salt. Set the cubes in a colander to drain for about 20 minutes.

2 Heat 2 tablespoons of the olive oil in a heavy-bottomed pot. Pat the eggplant dry, add to the pan, and cook over medium heat, stirring frequently, until golden. Add a bit more oil if the eggplant absorbs all the oil and sticks to the bottom of the pan. Remove the eggplant with a slotted spoon when done and set aside.

3 In the same pot, pour in the remaining 2 tablespoons of olive oil. Add the onions and cook for about 7 minutes, or until soft and translucent. Add the garlic, basil bouquet, chile flakes, and a bit more salt. Cook for 2 or 3 minutes, then stir in the peppers. Cook for a few more minutes, then stir in the summer squash. Cook for a few more minutes, then stir in the tomatoes. Cook for 10 minutes longer, then stir in the eggplant and cook for 10 to 15 minutes more, until all the vegetables are soft. Remove the bouquet of basil, pressing on it to extract all its flavors, and adjust the seasoning with salt.

4 Stir in the chopped basil leaves and more extra-virgin olive oil, to taste. Serve warm or cold.

# Gratin of Zucchini, Rice & Onions with Cheese

## FROM JULIA CHILD

While this gratin gives off the airs of a rich dish, it has no cream or butter and its luxurious base is largely vegetable water. And it's not because Julia Child was afraid of butter—it's just good that way. When you shred, salt, and squeeze a heap of zucchini dry, it sheds its water weight, leaving a tamed pile that won't flood your casserole, plus a lot of green, lightly salted liquid. Don't discard this.

This is one of those thoughtful, self-perpetuating recipes that could be designed into a very elegant flow chart. The zucchini juice that you squeeze out will form the base of a light béchamel, topped off with a little milk. Then you add just enough par-cooked rice to the gratin to soak up whatever juices remain and thicken the sauce, without asserting itself as empty filler.

Up to this point, you can cook ahead, refrigerating overnight even. Then, whenever you're ready for dinner, sprinkle on a bit of sharp Parmesan and bake until it's freckled and golden.

### Serves 6

2 to 2½ pounds (900g to 1.1kg) zucchini or other summer squash

½ cup (90g) white rice

1 cup (160g) minced onions

5 to 6 tablespoons olive oil

2 large cloves garlic, mashed or finely minced

2 tablespoons all-purpose flour

About 2½ cups (590ml) warm liquid (zucchini juices plus milk), heated

About ⅔ cups (65g) grated Parmesan cheese (save 2 tablespoons for later)

Salt and freshly ground black pepper

1 Shred the zucchini and drain, reserving the juices, as described on page 194. Meanwhile, drop the rice into boiling salted water, bring rapidly back to a boil, and boil for exactly 5 minutes; drain and set aside.

2 In a large (11-inch/28cm) frying pan, cook the onions slowly in 3 to 4 tablespoons oil for 8 to 10 minutes, until tender and translucent. Raise the heat slightly and stir for several minutes until very lightly browned. Stir in the grated and dried zucchini and garlic. Toss and turn for 5 to 6 minutes until the zucchini is almost tender. Sprinkle in the flour, stir over moderate heat for 2 minutes, and remove from the heat.

3 Gradually stir in the 2½ cups (590ml) of warm liquid (zucchini juices plus milk, heated gently in a pan; don't let it get so hot that the milk curdles). Make sure the flour is well blended and smooth. Put the pan over moderately high heat and bring to the simmer, stirring. Remove from the heat again, stir in the blanched rice and all but 2 tablespoons of the cheese. Taste very carefully for seasoning. Turn into a heavily buttered 6- to 8-cup (1.4 to 1.9L), flameproof

CONTINUED

baking and serving dish about 1½ inches (4cm) deep. Strew the remaining cheese on top and dribble the remaining 2 tablespoons olive oil over the cheese.

4 About half an hour before serving, preheat the oven to 425°F (220°C).

5 Bring the gratin to a simmer on top of stove (you can skip this if your baking dish isn't flameproof), then set the dish in upper third of the oven and bake until the tian is bubbling and top has browned nicely. The rice should absorb all the liquid. Serve hot or warm.

---

**GENIUS TIP**

Try adding a spoonful of raw rice when cooking purees, soups, and sauces to make them creamier, without adding more dairy or fat—much like its effect in this zucchini gratin. It sounds like one of the more joyless weight-loss tricks—and if you're catering to that crowd, this will play well—but it doesn't come from a place of deprivation.

The starch released from a tiny amount of rice amps up richness (think of risotto), while ensuring that none of the flavor is obscured. Michel Guérard adds rice to his root vegetable purees, cooking it along with the vegetables in milk before blending. Arborio rice makes Marcella Hazan's smothered cabbage soup feel almost extravagant. And in Paula Wolfert's leeks simmered in olive oil, she adds a tablespoon of rice halfway through, calling the dish "Mediterranean alchemy."

## Grated & Salted Zucchini
FROM JULIA CHILD

Shave the stem and the tip off each zucchini (or other summer squash), scrub the vegetable thoroughly but not harshly with a brush under cold running water to remove any clinging sand or dirt. If the vegetables are large, halve or quarter them. If the seeds are large and at all tough, and the surrounding flesh is coarse rather than moist and crisp, which is more often the case with yellow squashes and striped green cocozelles than with zucchini, cut out and discard the cores.

Rub the squash against the coarse side of a grater and place the grated flesh in a colander set over a bowl. For each 1 pound (2 cups/450g) of grated squash, toss with 1 teaspoon of salt, mixing thoroughly. Let the squash drain for 3 to 4 minutes, until you are ready to proceed.

Just before cooking, squeeze a handful of the squash dry and taste. If by any chance the squash is too salty, rinse in a large bowl of cold water, taste again; rinse and drain again, if necessary. Then squeeze gently by handfuls, letting juices run back into bowl. Dry on paper towels. Zucchini will not be fluffy; it is still dampish, but the excess liquid is out. The pale-green, slightly saline juice drained and squeezed out of the zucchini has a certain faint flavor that can find its uses in vegetable soups, canned soups, or vegetable sauces, in addition to this gratin.

# Potato Dominoes

## FROM FRANCIS MALLMANN

This technique from Argentine grilling master Francis Mallmann takes a very plain ingredient and glitzes it up, making starchy russet potatoes act like creamy Yukon Golds. It's not really about ingredients, and much more about shapes. The potatoes are squared off, sliced thinly, and fanned flat, before roasting crisp with clarified butter and salt, which—as in Nach Waxman's beef brisket (page 127)—makes every piece more like an end piece. The potatoes' natural starch fuses them together across the middle, while every edge gets brown and crisp.

Mallmann calls for the butter to be chilled so you can peel off little curls and smear them around. If you're in a hurry, you could instead just brush it on in melted form, but I like the effect of the slow-melting cold butter.

---

### GENIUS TIPS

This would leave an unconscionable amount of waste, if you were to throw the un-dominoed portions out. But don't! You can stash those end bits in the fridge in a bowl of water if you don't want to deal with them right away. Later, dry them off, toss them in oil and salt, and roast them off at 450°F (230°C) until tender and crisp, either in their haphazard state or cubed neatly (consider serving with the anchovy vinaigrette on page 183). Or boil the scraps and turn them into potato salad or soup or mash.

You can also try Mallman's technique with other roots or tubers (specifically, celery root or sweet potatoes), or baby potatoes.

### Serves 2 to 4

½ cup (115g) unsalted butter
4 Idaho or russet potatoes
Coarse salt

1 To make the clarified butter, slowly melt the butter in a small heavy saucepan over medium-low heat; do not stir. Remove from the heat and carefully spoon off and discard any foam from the top. Pour the clear liquid butter through a fine-mesh strainer, leaving behind the solids in the pan. Once cool, chill in the refrigerator. The clarified butter can be refrigerated for weeks.

2 To make the dominoes, preheat the oven to 400°F (200°C) with a rack in the center of the oven. Line a rimmed baking sheet with a silicone mat or use a nonstick baking sheet.

3 Cut off the two ends of one potato and reserve them. Trim the four sides of the potato to form an even brick. Slice the potato about ⅛ inch (3mm) thick on a mandoline, keeping the slices in order if you can (just like a line of shingled dominoes). Hold the stack of potato slices in the palm of one hand and use the other to shape them back into a brick, as you would a deck of cards. Lay the stack on its side on the baking sheet, and put the reserved potato ends, cut side down, at either end to keep the stack aligned. Then, with the palm of your hand, angle the slices slightly to resemble a line of dominoes that has tilted over. Adjust the end pieces to keep the stack in shape, and align the slices if necessary. Dot the top and sides with 1 tablespoon of the clarified butter. Sprinkle with salt to taste. Repeat with the remaining potatoes, keeping the stacks at least 2 inches (5cm) apart.

4 Bake for 40 minutes, or until the potatoes are browned on the edges and tender in the middle when tested with a skewer. Serve immediately.

# Desserts

# Strawberry Lemon Sorbet

## FROM RIVER CAFÉ

We're taught to zest our lemons carefully, to shear off just the thin yellow top coat that holds the citrusy perfume—as if some of the bitter, spongy white pith might sneak in and ruin everything. (And sometimes it does.)

But Ruth Rogers and Rose Gray, founders of the famed River Café in London, realized that, taken in the right proportions, some pith would add depth but not bitterness to a sweet dessert. So they told us to pulverize a whole chopped lemon, pith and all, and make strawberry sorbet out of it.

The process is enough to convince anyone, young or old, that the kitchen is an exciting place to be. Just three ingredients make a series of quick, colorful transformations, all in one food processor bowl. You get to see not only what strawberries look like as they surrender and slacken into a hot-pink soup, but also what happens when chopped lemon and sugar become one—going from sand to slush in just a few pulses. And because this effortlessly dissolves the sugar, you get to bypass making a simple syrup, a step often considered mandatory in sorbet recipes. In other words, this is a truly no-cook sorbet.

It's sweet and cold, with little pucker, and since you don't strain it, you get gleeful pops of strawberry seed and shreds of lemon rind (of course, you could always pass it through a strainer if textured sorbet isn't your thing, but for the true, rustic Rogers-and-Gray experience, don't).

Serve it as an invigorating dessert after something grilled and meaty. Or ease a scoop into a glass of seltzer or ginger ale and go sit in the sunshine.

**Makes 1½ quarts (1.4L)**

2 to 3 lemons, one seeded and roughly chopped, the others juiced

2 cups (400g) sugar

2 pounds (900g) strawberries, hulled

1 Place the lemon pieces into a food processor with the sugar, and pulse until combined. Pour into a bowl.

2 Puree the strawberries in a food processor and add to the lemon mixture, along with the juice of 1 lemon. Taste and add more juice as necessary. The flavor of the lemon should be intense but should not overpower the strawberries. Pour the mixture into an ice cream machine and churn until frozen. Serve immediately or transfer to a lidded container in the freezer until serving.

---

# One-Ingredient Banana Ice Cream & Fresh Peach Gelato

## ADAPTED FROM THE KITCHN & RUSS PARSONS

If you want fruity ice cream and don't have the machinery to pull it off, there are a couple of hacks you can use, with the help of a food processor (or high-speed blender).

*The Kitchn* made internet-famous one-ingredient banana ice cream (cut bananas, freeze a couple of hours until firm, and blend—the pectin whips up until it's as creamy as soft-serve). One bunch of bananas will serve 4 to 6.

Russ Parsons developed a similar recipe for fresh peach gelato with only two more ingredients, after learning the technique from Sicilian chef Ciccio Sultano: To serve 6 to 8, cut 3 pounds (1.4kg) peeled and pitted peaches into tiny pieces and freeze them in a single layer on a rimmed baking sheet for about 2 hours, until solid. Grind in a food processor with ¼ cup (50g) sugar, then add ½ cup (115g) mascarpone, crème fraîche, or yogurt, and pulse until the mixture is smooth. Taste and tweak. Freeze again, for 20 to 30 minutes, to firm it up before serving. If the ice cream freezes solid, process it briefly again.

# Strawberry Shortcakes

## FROM JAMES BEARD

As James Beard learned from his mother, the key to a better, more tender shortcake is egg yolks. This doesn't sound so strange, until you learn the yolks are from hard-boiled eggs. Crumbly cooked yolk dissolves into the crumb, adding richness without weighing down or gumming up the dough the way raw yolks would.

So, yes, there's one extra step: You have to boil a few eggs. But it's well worth it: This means the recipe is more forgiving than mixing in egg the usual way. Plus, you get a little pre-shortcake snack out of it.

For some reason, in his twenty-plus cookbooks, James Beard never published his mother's shortcake recipe himself. Lucky for us, he shared it with his friend Larry Forgione one night as the two were relaxing at Beard's townhouse. As Forgione tells it, Beard believed "there can be no dessert better, only fancier."

Serves 6

### BISCUITS

2 cups (250g) all-purpose flour

¼ cup plus 1 tablespoon (65g) sugar

1 tablespoon plus ½ teaspoon baking powder

6 tablespoons (85g) unsalted butter, chilled, cut into small cubes

2 hard-boiled egg yolks, pushed through a small mesh sieve

¾ cup (180ml) heavy cream, chilled

2 tablespoons unsalted butter, melted

### STRAWBERRIES

3 pints (1kg) fresh strawberries, washed, hulled, and halved or quartered, depending on size

2 tablespoons sugar

### WHIPPED CREAM

1 cup (240ml) heavy cream

1 tablespoon sugar

1 To make the biscuits, sift together the flour, ¼ cup (50g) of the sugar, and the baking powder into a bowl. Add the chilled butter pieces and, using your fingertips, work the butter into the flour mix until it has the consistency of coarse crumbs. Add the sieved hard-boiled egg yolks and the cream; gently mix until the dough just comes together.

2 Turn the dough onto a lightly floured board and gently knead to make a smooth dough (about two or three turns). Pat down the dough to make a 1-inch (2.5cm) thick round. Using a lightly floured 2½-inch (6.5cm) round cookie cutter, cut out shortcakes. Brush the tops with the melted butter and sprinkle with the remaining 1 tablespoon of sugar. Place the shortcakes on a plate lined with waxed paper or plastic wrap and refrigerate for an hour.

3 Preheat the oven to 350°F (175°C). Line a baking sheet with parchment paper.

4 Transfer the chilled shortcakes to the prepared baking sheet. Bake on the center rack of the oven for 12 to 15 minutes, until golden and firm to the touch. Remove from the oven and let cool slightly.

5 Meanwhile, prepare the strawberries and whipped cream. Put the strawberries in a glass bowl and add the sugar. Gently stir and let sit for 1 to 2 minutes.

6 Whip the cream and sugar together in a bowl until the cream just begins to thicken.

7 Using a fork or serrated knife, cut the shortcakes in half lengthwise. Place the bottom halves on dessert plates and generously spoon the macerated fruit and juices over them. Top with a heaping dollop of lightly whipped sweetened cream. Top with the top halves of the shortcakes and serve.

# Fresh Blueberry Pie

## FROM ROSE LEVY BERANBAUM

A blueberry is just a sack of tart-sweet juice, barely contained by a thin, taut orb of skin. It's nature's tiniest water balloon, and like any good water balloon, it wasn't designed to last. So when we want to bake blueberries into a pie, they're going to swell through their skins and surrender all their juice, which then needs to be jammed up with sugar and thickeners to sop up all that's been freed. There's nothing necessarily wrong with that—throw on a scoop of vanilla ice cream, and it's not *not* going to get eaten, but there's another sort of blueberry pie. It uses a lighter touch, managing to preserve fresh blueberries in their natural state and drape them in a sauce—made, of course, from more burst blueberries.

A quarter of your berry haul gets cooked in a little water until the berries explode (about 3 minutes). As they're bursting into a syrupy pulp, you whisk in a slurry of cornstarch and water, plus lemon and salt. The rest of your berries get folded in next, off the heat, and they light up—from a low dusty blue to shimmering indigo in seconds. This blueberry jumble goes into your prebaked pie crust and you're done— you won't cook it again. The only hard part is waiting two hours to eat it.

### GENIUS TIP

You can use your go-to single pie crust here, or I've included Beranbaum's recipe, which has all sorts of clever tricks. She uses pastry flour and vinegar for less gluten development and a more delicate crust, baking powder for a little extra lift. She freezes part of the butter, and bashes it into the flour with a rolling pin to make long, ragged flakes in the pastry. She wrote the *Pie and Pastry Bible,* after all, so she knows what she's doing.

### Serves 6

#### BASIC FLAKY PIE CRUST

8 tablespoons (115g) unsalted butter, cold

1⅓ cups plus 4 teaspoons pastry flour or 1⅓ cups (dip-and-sweep method, see page 229) bleached all-purpose flour (185g)

¼ teaspoon salt

⅛ teaspoon nonaluminum baking powder

2½ to 3½ tablespoons ice water

1½ teaspoons cider vinegar (optional)

#### FRESH BLUEBERRY FILLING

1 tablespoon egg white, lightly beaten (optional)

4 cups (590g) blueberries, rinsed and dried

½ liquid cup (120ml) plus 2 tablespoons water, divided

2 tablespoons cornstarch

½ cup (100g) sugar

1 teaspoon fresh lemon juice

Pinch of salt

1½ cups (360ml) whipped cream (optional)

1 **To make the crust,** divide the butter into two parts, about two thirds to one third, or 5 tablespoons and 3 tablespoons. Cut the butter into ¾-inch (2cm) cubes. Wrap each portion of butter with plastic wrap, then refrigerate the larger amount and freeze the smaller for at least 30 minutes. Place the flour, salt, and baking powder in a reclosable gallon-size freezer bag and freeze for at least 30 minutes.

2 Place a mixing bowl in the freezer to chill. Place the chilled flour mix in another bowl and whisk to combine.

3 Use a pastry cutter or rub the mixture between your fingers to blend the larger portion of the butter into the flour until it resembles coarse meal. Spoon the mixture, together with the cold butter from the freezer,

CONTINUED

# Fresh Blueberry Pie
## Continued

into a reclosable gallon-size freezer bag. Expel any air from the bag and close it. Use a rolling pin to flatten the butter into flakes. Place the bag in the freezer for at least 10 minutes, or until the butter is very firm.

4 Transfer the mixture to the chilled bowl, scraping the sides of the bag. Set the bag aside. Sprinkle the ice water and vinegar onto the mixture, tossing it lightly with a rubber spatula. Spoon the loose mixture back into the plastic bag.

5 Holding both ends of the bag opening with your fingers, knead the mixture by alternately pressing it, from the outside of the bag, with the knuckles and heels of your hands until the mixture holds together in one piece and feels slightly stretchy when pulled.

6 Wrap the dough with plastic wrap, flatten it into a disc, and refrigerate for at least 45 minutes, preferably overnight. This dough can be stored, refrigerated, for up to 2 days; frozen, for up to 3 months.

7 Remove the dough from the refrigerator. If necessary, allow it to sit for about 10 minutes or until it is soft enough to roll. Using a pastry cloth and sleeve rubbed with flour or two sheets of plastic wrap lightly sprinkled with flour, roll the dough ⅛ inch (3mm) thick or less and large enough to cut a 13-inch (33cm) circle. Use an expandable flan ring or a cardboard template and a sharp knife as a guide to cut out the circle. Transfer the dough to the pie pan, fold under the excess, and crimp the border using a fork or your fingers (or just fold it under). Cover it loosely and refrigerate it for a minimum of 1 hour and a maximum of 24 hours. Preheat the oven to 425°F (220°C) at least 20 minutes before baking.

8 Line the pastry with parchment paper, pleating it as necessary so it fits into the pan, and fill it with rice or dried beans. Bake for 20 minutes. Carefully lift out the rice or beans with the parchment. With a fork, prick the bottom and sides, and bake for 5 to 10 minutes, until the crust is pale golden. Check after 3 minutes and prick any bubbles that may have formed.

9 Cool the crust on a rack for 3 minutes, so it is no longer piping hot, then (optionally) brush the bottom and sides with the egg white; this will help keep the bottom crust from getting soggy.

10 **To make the filling,** measure out 1 cup (150g) of the blueberries, choosing the softest ones. Put them in a saucepan together with ½ cup (120ml) of the water. Cover and bring to a boil.

11 Meanwhile, in a small bowl, whisk together the cornstarch and the remaining 2 tablespoons of water. Set it aside.

12 When the water and blueberries have come to a boil, lower the heat and simmer, stirring constantly for 3 to 4 minutes, until the blueberries start to burst and the juices begin to thicken. Stirring constantly, add the cornstarch mixture, sugar, lemon juice, and salt. Simmer for a minute or until the mixture becomes translucent. Immediately remove it from the heat and quickly fold in the remaining 3 cups of blueberries.

13 Spoon the mixture into the baked pie shell and allow to sit at room temperature for at least 2 hours before serving. When set, the berries will remain very juicy but will not flow out of the crust. Serve with whipped cream, if desired. This pie can be stored at room temperature for up to 2 days (without the whipped cream).

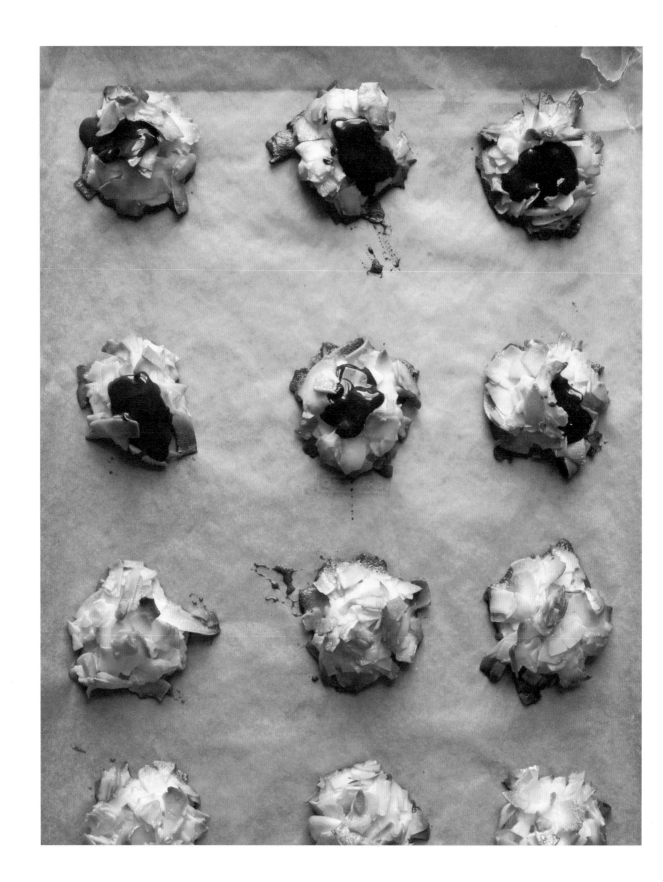

# New Classic Coconut Macaroons

## FROM ALICE MEDRICH

What seems in part to define macaroons is what they usually lack: flour (which makes them perfect for Passover observers and gluten avoiders). Alice Medrich's macaroons do fall in line here, relying on little more than coconut for heft, and a brew of egg whites and sugar to hold it all together.

But she's famously a little wild with her desserts and developed this recipe not with the standard bag of soft, sweetened shreds in mind, but those wide, sloping unsweetened shavings, often called coconut chips and sold at health food stores. (They also pop up in genius granola, page 15.)

Working with a different cut of coconut is enough to completely change the outcome. The tiny wings of coconut toast up crisp and brown, while the inside layers stay soft and discrete.

### Makes about 22 cookies

4 large egg whites

3½ cups (210g) unsweetened coconut chips or 3 cups (255g) sweetened, dried shredded coconut

¾ cup (150g) sugar

2 teaspoons pure vanilla extract (available kosher for Passover, or can be omitted)

Slightly rounded ¼ teaspoon salt

1 Combine all of the ingredients in a large heatproof mixing bowl, preferably stainless steel because the mixture will heat faster than in glass. Set the bowl directly in a wide skillet of barely simmering water (if your bowl bobs in the water, simply pour some water out). Stir the mixture with a silicone spatula, scraping the bottom to prevent burning, until the mixture is very hot to the touch, and the egg whites have thickened slightly and turned from translucent to opaque, 5 to 7 minutes. Set the batter aside for 30 minutes to let the coconut absorb more of the goop.

2 Preheat the oven to 350°F (175°C). Position racks in the upper and lower thirds of the oven. Line two cookie sheets with parchment paper.

3 Using 2 tablespoons of batter, make attractive heaps 2 inches (5cm) apart on the cookie sheets. Bake for about 5 minutes, just until the coconut tips begin to color, rotating the pans from top to bottom and from front to back halfway through the baking time to ensure even baking.

4 Lower the oven temperature to 325°F (165°C) and bake for 10 to 15 minutes, until the cookies are a beautiful cream and gold with deeper brown edges, again rotating the pans from top to bottom and from front to back halfway through the baking time. If the coconut tips are browning too fast, lower the heat to 300°F (150°C). Set the pans or just the liners on racks to cool. Let cool completely before gently peeling the parchment away from each cookie.

5 The cookies are best on the day they are baked—the exterior is crisp and chewy and the interior soft and moist. Although the crispy edges will soften, the cookies remain delicious stored in an airtight container for 4 to 5 days.

---

### UPGRADES

Chocolate-Topped Coconut Macaroons: While the macaroons are still hot, top each with a little piece of your favorite milk or dark chocolate. Or drizzle a little melted chocolate over each cookie.

Coconut Macaroons with Lime Zest and Cinnamon: Stir 1½ to 2 teaspoons freshly grated lime zest into the batter before scooping it. Using a fine grater or Microplane, grate a little cinnamon stick over the cookies just before serving.

# Sweet Corn & Black Raspberry Ice Cream

FROM JENI BRITTON BAUER

An eggy custard base has a nasty habit of muting other flavors in ice cream. The butterfat in cream, on the other hand, will melt and bloom as soon as it hits your tongue—loud and clear, you're tasting vanilla, or roasted pistachio, or dark chocolate. So Jeni Britton Bauer of Jeni's Splendid Ice Creams in Columbus, Ohio, developed an eggless formula to put the butterfat in charge, while keeping gritty ice crystals at bay, too—all with the help of readily available baking-aisle staples.

Most of her ice cream recipes start with the same comforting step, prepping three bowls: a lump of soft cream cheese whisked with salt; a cornstarch and milk slurry; and an ice bath, with a sturdy Ziploc bag bobbing in it, waiting to cool down your base fast. This is like food chemistry lab for preschoolers.

Her sweet corn ice cream with pockets of black raspberry sauce alone is worth the price of an ice cream maker (which is cheaper than you'd think). But Bauer's genius is also in giving you a blueprint so you can go your own way. It can be as simple as steeping a vanilla bean, or as complicated as you like.

**Makes a generous 1 quart (1L)**

### BLACK RASPBERRY SAUCE

2 cups (300g) raspberries, black raspberries, and/or blackberries

1 cup (200g) sugar

### SWEET CORN ICE CREAM

1 ear sweet corn, husked

2 cups (475ml) whole milk

1 tablespoon plus 1 teaspoon cornstarch

1½ ounces (45g/3 tablespoons) cream cheese, softened

¼ teaspoon fine sea salt

1¼ cups (300ml) heavy cream

⅔ cup (135g) sugar

2 tablespoons light corn syrup

1 **To make the sauce,** combine the berries and sugar in a small saucepan and bring to a boil over medium-high heat. Continue boiling, stirring occasionally, until it reaches 220°F/105°C (5 to 8 minutes). Let cool slightly, then force through a sieve to remove the seeds. (Or leave a few seeds in there just to prove you made it.) Refrigerate until cold before using. Makes about 1¼ cups (300ml).

2 **To make the ice cream,** slice the kernels from the corn cob, then "milk" the cob by scraping it with the back of your knife to extract the liquid; reserve the kernels and liquid. Mix about 2 tablespoons of the milk with the cornstarch in a small bowl to make a smooth slurry. Whisk the cream cheese and salt in a medium bowl until smooth. Fill a large bowl with ice and water.

3 Combine the remaining milk, the cream, sugar, corn and juices, and corn syrup in a 4-quart (3.8L) saucepan, bring to a rolling boil over medium-high heat, and boil for 4 minutes. Remove from the heat and force the mixture through a sieve into a bowl, keeping the corn "cases" behind. Return the mixture to the saucepan and gradually whisk in the cornstarch slurry. Bring back to a boil over medium-high heat and cook, stirring with a heatproof spatula, until slightly thickened, about 1 minute. Remove from the heat.

4 Gradually whisk the hot milk mixture into the cream cheese until smooth. Pour the mixture into a 1-gallon (3.8L) Ziploc freezer bag and submerge the sealed bag in the ice bath. Let stand, adding more ice as necessary, until cold, about 30 minutes.

5 Pour the ice cream base into your ice cream maker and spin until thick and creamy. Pack the ice cream into a storage container, alternating it with layers of the black raspberry sauce and ending with a spoonful of sauce; do not mix. Press a sheet of parchment directly against the surface, and seal with an airtight lid. Freeze in the coldest part of your freezer until firm, at least 4 hours.

# Chocolate Mousse

FROM HERVÉ THIS

Every chocolate book and pastry chef teaches us to never let water get near melting chocolate: It will seize and crumble, and ruin dessert. But Hervé This—the French chemist who invented the study of (and the very phrase) molecular gastronomy—figured out how to mix the unmixable and turn them into chocolate mousse.

It also happens to be the simplest way to make mousse at home: Melt chocolate with water, then cool it over an ice bath and whisk till you have mousse.

Like other emulsions (vinaigrette, aïoli), as you whip, microscopic bits of water get suspended in the fat (here: cocoa butter), thickening it and making it seem creamier. The cooling chocolate crystallizes around the air bubbles, just like whipped cream, to make a remarkably stable foam, a.k.a. mousse.

The best thing about this is that it tastes like pure, unobstructed chocolate, without cream or egg to confuse the issue. (It also happens to be vegan, if you use dark chocolate without any added milk.)

This all happens fast as the mixture cools, so chances are you'll go too far on your first try and the mousse may stiffen up beyond the point you'd wanted. But if this happens, Mr. This is unfazed—he has you return the chocolate mixture to the pan, melt it, and start over (see note).

---

**GENIUS TIP**

Once you have the rhythm of making this mousse down, you can flavor it as you wish with liqueurs or coffee or spices, sweeten it to your liking, or just keep it dark and intense.

**Serves 4**

¾ cup (180ml) water

8 ounces (225g) chocolate (I use bittersweet chocolate that's 70 percent cacao—choose a high-quality chocolate you love), broken into pieces

Ice cubes

Whipped cream, for topping (optional; page 236)

1 Simply pour the water into a saucepan over medium-low heat (the water can be improved from the gastronomic point of view if it is flavored with orange juice, for example, or cassis puree—just replace some of the water with an equal amount of the flavorful liquid). Then, add the chocolate and whisk it in as it melts. The result is a homogenous sauce.

2 Put the saucepan in a bowl partly filled with ice cubes (or pour into another bowl over the ice so it will chill faster), then whisk the chocolate sauce, either manually with a whisk or with an electric mixer (if using an electric mixer, watch closely—it will thicken faster). Whisking creates large air bubbles in the sauce, which steadily thickens. After a while strands of chocolate form inside the loops of the whisk. Pour or spoon immediately into ramekins, small bowls, or jars and let set.

NOTE: Three things can go wrong. Here's how to fix them. If your chocolate doesn't contain enough fat and won't form a mousse, melt the mixture again, add more chocolate, and then whisk it again. If the mousse is not light enough, melt the mixture again, add more water, and whisk it once more. If you whisk it too much, so that it becomes grainy, simply melt the mixture and whisk it again, adding nothing.

3 Serve immediately, or refrigerate until serving. Top with whipped cream, if desired.

# Purple Plum Torte

## FROM MARIAN BURROS

Marian Burros published this torte recipe in the *New York Times* in 1982, bringing it back by request every September until 1989, rarely varying a thing. By the last year, the headline was "Once More (Sigh), The Plum Torte."

Fifteen years later, when Amanda Hesser polled the *Times's* readership for their favorite (and most stained) recipes for *The Essential New York Times Cookbook*, this one still had more than three times the votes of any other.

Where does the attachment come from? It may be that the recipe is simple in method and flawless in results: The plums are perched in a batter that puffs up elegantly around them. The instructions also allow a rare versatility for a baked good—namely, how to balance the relative sweetness or sourness of your plums (with more or less sugar and lemon strewn across the top). Why mess with a good thing? Many of Burros's readers saw no reason to.

---

**GENIUS TIP**

Use peak-season plums if you've got them, but this is also a good place to stick any tart, underripe plums (or other stone fruits) you wouldn't bother eating out of hand. Baking improves their character.

**Serves 8**

¾ cup (150g) sugar, plus more for topping

½ cup (115g) unsalted butter, softened

1 cup (125g) unbleached all-purpose flour, sifted

1 teaspoon baking powder

Pinch of salt (optional)

2 large eggs

24 halves small, pitted purple plums (or as many as will fit on your cake)

Fresh lemon juice, for topping

Ground cinnamon, for topping

1 Preheat the oven to 350°F (175°C).

2 Cream the sugar and butter in a bowl. Add the flour, baking powder, salt, and eggs, and beat well. Spoon the batter into a springform of 8, 9, or 10 inches (20, 23, or 25cm). Place the plum halves skin side up on top of the batter. Sprinkle lightly with sugar and lemon juice, depending on the sweetness of the fruit. Sprinkle with (about) 1 teaspoon of cinnamon, depending on how much you like cinnamon.

3 Bake for 40 to 50 minutes, approximately, until a cake tester inserted in the center comes out clean. Remove and cool; refrigerate or freeze if desired (but first, double-wrap the torte in foil, place in a plastic bag, and seal). Or cool to lukewarm, and serve. To serve a torte that has been frozen, defrost and reheat it briefly at 300°F (150°C).

# Dense Chocolate Loaf Cake

## FROM NIGELLA LAWSON

This is a good cake to keep lying around—for roaming family members who need to be kept happy between mealtimes, for neighbors who swoop in unannounced, for you.

It's a chocolate cake that's full of nuance and personality, damp and puddinglike within, with caramel-crisp edges. Where most loaf cakes are domed, sturdy, and evenly crumbed, this one is slumped and squidgy (from the British, meaning "soft, spongy, and moist").

That's thanks to a generous amount of dark brown sugar that arms the cake with loads of moisture. There is also the rather unusual step of starting with creamed soft butter and brown sugar and ending with spoonfuls of boiling water interspersed with leavened flour, making a surprisingly runny batter. It is this creaming and partially melting process that makes the final product resemble a cake, a steamed pudding, and a fudgy brownie all at once.

It also causes this cake to collapse in a slightly different way every time you bake it. Embrace it—it's this collapse that gives the cake its glorious denseness. If you're concerned by the looks of it (Heidi Swanson nicknamed her spelt-based version "chocolate ugly cake"), you can distract with crème fraîche, whipped cream, or cold cream cheese, the way Lawson likes it.

### Makes 8 to 10 slices

1 cup (225g) soft unsalted butter

1⅔ cups (375g) packed dark brown or dark muscovado sugar

2 large eggs, beaten

1 teaspoon pure vanilla extract

4 ounces (100g) best bittersweet chocolate, melted

1⅓ cups (200g) all-purpose flour

1 teaspoon baking soda

1 cup plus 2 tablespoons (250ml) boiling water

1 Preheat the oven to 375°F (190°C). Put a baking sheet on a lower rack in case of sticky drips later. Grease a 9 by 5-inch (23 by 13cm) loaf pan and line with parchment paper. The lining is important as this is a very damp cake; use parchment paper or one of those loaf-pan-shaped paper liners.

2 Cream the butter and brown sugar, either with a wooden spoon or with an electric mixer, then add the eggs and vanilla, beating in well. Next, fold in the melted and now slightly cooled chocolate, taking care to blend well but being careful not to overbeat. You want the ingredients combined. You don't want a light, airy mass.

3 Mix the flour and baking soda and gently add the flour mixture to the batter, alternately spoon by spoon with the boiling water until you have a smooth and fairly liquid batter. Pour into the lined loaf pan. (Note: Don't let this batter come closer than 1 inch/2.5cm from the rim of the loaf pan or it risks overflowing. Pour any excess into a smaller cake or muffin pan.) Bake for 30 minutes.

4 Turn the oven down to 325°F (170°C) and continue to bake for another 15 minutes. The cake will still be a bit squidgy inside, so an inserted cake tester or skewer won't come out completely clean.

5 Place the loaf pan on a rack and leave it to get completely cold before turning it out. (Lawson often leaves it for a day or so; like gingerbread, it improves.) Don't worry if it sinks in the middle; indeed, it will do so because it's such a dense and damp cake.

# Marie-Hélène's Apple Cake

## FROM DORIE GREENSPAN

Cookbook author Dorie Greenspan built this recipe—an apple cake that's more apples than cake—from the memory of one served by her friend Marie-Hélène, the frustrating sort of excellent cook who doesn't measure or slow down enough to record her own recipes.

Greenspan is emphatic that you choose four different kinds of apple, since they each behave differently when baked. Some sweeten and collapse; some stay structural and tart. They do all the work of making the cake interesting, without a crumble, or nuts, or even cinnamon. This also means that the cake stands to come out a little bit different every time. If that makes you nervous, you could make a note of the apple varieties that work best for you, but know that apples cobbled together with gently boozed up, custardy cake are going to be well received, no matter what. Serve the cake alone, or with soft whipped cream. Greenspan says, "Marie-Hélène served her cake with cinnamon ice cream and it was a terrific combination."

### Serves 8

¾ cup (95g) all-purpose flour

¾ teaspoon baking powder

Pinch of salt

4 large apples (if you can, choose four different kinds)

2 large eggs

¾ cup (150g) sugar

3 tablespoons dark rum

½ teaspoon pure vanilla extract

½ cup (115g) unsalted butter, melted and cooled

1 Center a rack in the oven, and preheat the oven to 350°F (175°C). Generously butter an 8-inch (20cm) springform pan and put it on a baking sheet lined with a silicone baking mat or parchment paper.

2 Whisk the flour, baking powder, and salt together in small bowl.

3 Peel the apples, cut them in halves and remove the cores. Cut into 1- to 2-inch (2.5 to 5cm) chunks.

4 In a bowl, beat the eggs with a whisk until they're foamy. Pour in the sugar and whisk for a minute or so to blend. Whisk in the rum and vanilla. Whisk in half the flour mixture and when it is incorporated, add half the melted butter, followed by the rest of the flour mixture and the remaining butter, mixing gently after each addition so that you have a smooth, rather thick batter. Switch to a rubber spatula and fold in the apples, turning the fruit so that it's coated with batter. Scrape the mix into the pan and poke it around a little with the spatula so that it's evenish.

5 Slide the pan into the oven and bake for 50 to 60 minutes, until the top of the cake is golden brown and a knife inserted deep into the center comes out clean; the cake may pull away from the sides of the pan. Transfer to a cooling rack and let rest for 5 minutes.

6 Carefully run a blunt knife around the edges of the cake and remove the sides of the springform pan. (Open the springform slowly, and before it's fully opened, make sure there aren't any apples stuck to it.) Allow the cake to cool until it is just slightly warm or at room temperature. If you want to remove the cake from the bottom of the springform pan, wait until the cake is almost cooled, then run a long spatula between the cake and the pan, cover the top of the cake with a piece of parchment or waxed paper, and invert it onto a rack. Carefully remove the bottom of the pan and turn the cake over onto a serving dish.

7 The cake can be served warm or at room temperature, and will keep for about 2 days at room temperature. Greenspan's husband says it gets more comforting with each passing day. However long you keep the cake, it's best not to cover it—it's too moist. Leave the cake on its plate and just press a piece of plastic wrap or wax paper against the cut surfaces.

# Pumpkin Pie

FROM META GIVEN

When Judy Hesser (mom of Amanda) told me that her favorite pumpkin pie recipe, from *Meta Given's Modern Encyclopedia of Cooking,* involves cooking down canned pumpkin to caramelize it, that alone was enough to sell me. It sounded like a pie with guts, that wouldn't phone in the pumpkin flavor and bury it under lots of spice. But the genius of the recipe is much more than that.

You don't have to blind bake the crust (that is, bake it before filling and, usually, baking again, page 205). You use fresh milk and cream instead of evaporated milk, with predictably richer results. And because you blast it at 400°F (200°C) the whole time, it bakes in 25 minutes—less than half the time of your average back-of-the-can recipe. (If you're wondering how a custard pie can sustain such abuse, I credit the cream and the chilled pie shell.)

Caramelizing the pumpkin doesn't make it stick to the dry saucepan like you may be worrying it will; it's moist enough that it basically keeps deglazing itself. And the caramelizing does everything you'd hope for the flavor: intensely, proudly pumpkin.

Rich as it is, you may only want a small slice, and you might not even need the whipped cream, but make sure you have a bowlful, just to be safe (page 236). And—oh well!—that just means more left to eat cold for breakfast the next day.

## Serves 6

1¾ cups (425g) canned or fresh cooked pumpkin puree
¾ cup (150g) sugar
½ teaspoon salt
1 teaspoon ground cinnamon
½ teaspoon ground ginger
2 large eggs
1 cup (240ml) heavy cream
½ cup (120ml) milk
Unbaked, unpricked, chilled 9-inch (23cm) pie shell (store-bought or homemade, page 205)

1 Preheat the oven to 400°F (200°C).

2 Turn the pumpkin into a saucepan and stir frequently over moderate, direct heat for 10 minutes until somewhat dry and slightly caramelized. Remove from the heat but keep hot.

3 Mix thoroughly together the sugar, salt, cinnamon, and ginger, and stir into the hot pumpkin. Beat the eggs, add the cream and milk, and beat into the pumpkin mixture until smooth.

4 Pour immediately into the unpricked pastry-lined pie pan and bake for 25 to 30 minutes, until the pastry is golden brown and only a 1-inch (2.5cm) circle in the center of the filling remains liquid. Cool thoroughly on a wire rack before cutting.

NOTE: Perfectly baked pumpkin pie has no cracks on its surface. Baking hot filling in a chilled crust at 400°F (200°C) for 25 to 30 minutes produces a smooth, shiny, good-textured custard and a well-baked crust free from soaking. But if your pie dish is thicker glass or ceramic instead of metal, or you loathe underdone bottom crust, you might still want to blind bake it a little. Here's what I'd recommend: Blind bake at 350°F (175°C) with the pastry shell lined with parchment paper and filled with baking beans or weights until the sides are dry and firm, 10 to 15 minutes. Remove the parchment and weights, then bake until completely dry and firm (including bottom crust) and starting to turn golden, 5 to 10 minutes more. Cool thoroughly. Then watch the pie closely as it bakes with the filling—it might be done early, since the cold raw crust isn't there to protect it. And if the edges of the filling are starting to look wrinkled while the middle is very jiggly, turn the heat down to 350°F (175°C).

## GENIUS TIPS

In making pastry, you have an ally you might not have realized: your box grater. Grating a frozen stick of butter makes long flakes that distribute quickly and evenly into flour while staying cold. Or you can go one step further and grate the chilled dough, a trick April Bloomfield uses to skip rolling out crust for her banoffee pie and Joanne Chang does for the shortbread crumb topping for her raspberry bars.

# Molasses Cookies

## FROM THE SILVER PALATE

The Silver Palate's molasses cookie is one that's spiced and sweetened delicately so it doesn't feel out of place outside of December. It's like a subtler, softer gingersnap that you could just as easily serve next to an iced coffee or bowl of plums or pot of rhubarb jam as you could a glass of eggnog.

The dough is also exceedingly quick to make (you could be eating one 30 minutes from now), and they bake up flat and chewy, which means they're the perfect ice cream sandwich cookie. Some suggestions for ice cream middles are at right and on pages 200 and 213.

---

## Cheater Soft-Serve Ice Cream
### ADAPTED FROM JOHN T. EDGE

You can fake having a fancy, commercial soft serve machine with this trick: Soften 3 cups (400g) of vanilla ice cream. Whip ½ cup (120ml) of heavy cream to soft peaks, then add a tablespoon of sugar and ¼ teaspoon of pure vanilla extract, and finish whisking the cream to stiff peaks. Using a rubber spatula, stir in the soft ice cream until well combined. Scrape into a large, resealable freezer bag and freeze until soft serve-like and semifirm, about 4 hours.

When it's time to serve, remove the bag from the freezer and, if necessary, knead the bag to soften the ice cream. (It will be cold, but you can knead through a kitchen towel to protect your hands.) Cut off a corner of the bag to pipe ice cream into a cone or a bowl. Makes 1 quart (1L).

**Makes 24 very large flat cookies**

12 tablespoons (1½ sticks/170g) sweet butter
1 cup (200g) granulated sugar
¼ cup (60ml) molasses
1 egg
1¾ cups (220g) unbleached all-purpose flour
½ teaspoon ground cloves
½ teaspoon ground ginger
1 teaspoon ground cinnamon
½ teaspoon salt
½ teaspoon baking soda

1 Preheat oven to 350°F (175°C).

2 Melt butter, add sugar and molasses, and mix thoroughly. Lightly beat egg and add to butter mixture; blend well.

3 Sift flour with spices, salt, and baking soda, and add to first mixture; mix. Batter will be wet.

4 Lay a sheet of foil on a cookie sheet. Drop tablespoons of cookie batter on foil, leaving 3 inches (7.5cm) between the cookies. These will spread during the baking.

5 Bake until cookies start to darken, 8 to 10 minutes. Remove from oven while still soft. Let cool on foil.

# Fresh Ginger Cake

## FROM SYLVIA THOMPSON

Sometimes baked goods in the spiced genre can taste a bit like a candle shop, or a stale corner of the pantry. No wonder they're less popular than chocolate and fruit and custard desserts: They feel less alive. All spice cake needs is new blood: A big dose of fresh ginger will give you infinitely more brightness and fire than a dormant jar of the ground kind.

Cookbook author Sylvia Thompson's is the simplest and best of the fresh ginger cakes I've tried. She calls for fresh ginger the size of an egg, grated medium fine. There's no need to even peel it. Most of ginger's unsavory fibrous bits, inside and out, break down under the grater and fade into the cake. She also kindly gives guidelines for baking in virtually any cake pan you want, and for serving warm or cool.

Serves at least 8

QUATRE ÉPICES
1 tablespoon ground white pepper
¼ teaspoon ground cloves
1 teaspoon ground ginger
1 teaspoon grated nutmeg

½ cup (115g) unsalted butter, plus a little softened for the pan
½ cup (120ml) cool water
½ cup (110g) firmly packed light brown sugar
¼ cup (60ml) light molasses
¼ cup (60ml) dark corn syrup
1 extra-large egg
Fresh ginger the size of an egg, grated medium-fine
1½ cups (190g) all-purpose flour, plus a little more for the pan
1 teaspoon baking soda
¼ teaspoon salt
Sifted confectioners' sugar or sweet potato caramel (page 230) for the top

1 Preheat the oven to 350°F (175°C). Choose any baking dish with a 6- to 8-cup (1.4L to 1.9L) capacity (Thompson uses an 8-inch/20cm square). Brush with butter and dust with flour.

2 **To make the *quatre épices*,** stir together all spices. The spice blend will keep in an airtight container for 6 months.

3 Melt the butter in the water either in a largish saucepan over medium heat or in a glass mixing bowl in the microwave. Do not let the water boil (and thus evaporate).

4 To the butter and water, whisk in the brown sugar, molasses, and corn syrup, and then the egg. Whisk in the ginger, discarding any long strings the whisk brings up. Add the flour, baking soda, 1 teaspoon of the *quatre épices*, and salt. Whisk a minute or two until the lumps dissolve. Pour into the pan. Rap gently on the counter to knock out any air bubbles.

5 Bake until a fine skewer thrust in the center comes out clean and the top, when tapped, springs back, about 35 minutes for a square (or ring or round), less for a shallower rectangle, more for a deeper loaf. Gently turn out onto a doily-lined dish to serve warm or onto a rack to serve cool. Finish with sifted confectioners' sugar or serve with sweet potato caramel (page 230) or chocolate frosting, as food writer Laurie Colwin did.

"But why has this cake an almost mystical quality? I invariably find myself baking it to celebrate significant occasions in my life. I think it is the deep down comfort of the dark sweeteners and knowing instinctively that ginger's heat has had a pull on cultures universally." —S.T.

# Whole Wheat Chocolate Chip Cookies

FROM KIM BOYCE

Sure, you might want to start using whole grain flours in all your favorite baked goods—they're a purer form of the ingredients, we're told they're good for us, they have flavor and texture in spades. But we need guidance. Baking is simply more forgiving with refined, consistent, industrial products. Luckily, pastry chef Kim Boyce understands whole grain flours, but also knows what a great cookie tastes like.

In her all-whole wheat chocolate chip cookie recipe, the grain isn't there just for health but also for flavor—so much so that she has you add back in any bigger pieces of grain that get caught in the sifter. The integrity of the grain is (almost) the whole point.

**Makes about 20 cookies**

3 cups (360g) whole wheat flour (see Genius Tip)

1½ teaspoons baking powder

1 teaspoon baking soda

1½ teaspoons kosher salt

1 cup (230g) cold unsalted butter, cut into ½-inch (1.3cm) pieces

1 cup (220g) packed dark brown sugar

1 cup (200g) granulated sugar

2 large eggs

2 teaspoons pure vanilla extract

8 ounces (225g) bittersweet chocolate, roughly chopped into ¼- and ½-inch (6mm and 1.3cm) pieces

1 Place two racks in the upper and lower thirds of the oven and preheat to 350°F (175°C). Line two baking sheets with parchment. Although you can butter the sheets instead, parchment is useful for these cookies because the large chunks of chocolate can stick to the pan.

2 Sift the flour, baking powder, baking soda, and salt into a large bowl, pouring back into the bowl any bits of grain or other ingredients that may remain in the sifter.

3 Put the butter and brown and white sugars in the bowl of a standing mixer fitted with a paddle attachment. With the mixer on low speed, mix just until the butter and sugars are blended, about 2 minutes. Use a spatula to scrape down the sides of the bowl. Add the eggs, one at a time, mixing until each is combined. Mix in the vanilla. Add the flour mixture to the bowl and blend on low speed until the flour is barely combined, about 30 seconds. Scrape down the sides and bottom of the bowl.

4 Add the chocolate all at once to the batter. Mix on low speed until the chocolate is evenly combined. Use a spatula to scrape down the sides and bottom of the bowl, then scrape the batter out onto a work surface, and use your hands to fully incorporate all the ingredients.

5 Scoop mounds of dough about 3 tablespoons in size onto the baking sheets, leaving 3 inches (7.5cm) between them, or about six to a sheet.

6 Bake the cookies for 16 to 20 minutes, rotating the sheets halfway through, until the cookies are evenly dark brown. Transfer the cookies, still on the parchment paper, to the counter to cool, and repeat with the remaining dough. These cookies are best eaten warm from the oven or later that same day. They'll keep in an airtight container for up to 3 days.

---

**GENIUS TIP**

Because whole wheat flour is fairly unforgiving, it's especially important to use the spoon-and-sweep method to avoid over-filling your measuring cup. Stir the flour in its container to loosen it, spoon it lightly into the cup, then sweep off the excess with the flat side of a knife or bench scraper. (In the dip-and-sweep method, dip the measuring cup directly in the container, for a more compacted result.)

# Caramelized White Chocolate

## FROM VALRHONA

Past the pale, sweet exterior of white chocolate lie three ingredients with a lot of potential—sugar, milk, and fat (in the form of cocoa butter). What happens when you expose these to enough heat? The sugars toast and you get caramel.

How to enjoy it (besides out of the jar): Melt it into hot chocolate. Whisk in some hot cream to make a ganache, then sandwich it between cookies. For a grown-up version of Magic Shell, stir in vegetable or coconut oil (about a tablespoon to 8 ounces/225g of chocolate, melted), pour over ice cream, and sprinkle on flaky salt.

Alternatively, if you keep roasting until it seizes into crumbles, don't worry. It is completely salvageable and, in fact, it may be a handier form to keep around for baking (into the whole wheat chocolate chip cookies on page 229, for example). You can freely toss handfuls into scones, brownies, or banana cake (page 5). You can also force it to become completely smooth with the aid of a blender or a fine-mesh strainer if you wish; just warm with a little cream or neutral oil in a double boiler, then either blend or strain.

**Makes about 1½ cups (360ml)**

1 pound (450g) white chocolate
Sea salt, to taste

1 Preheat oven to 265°F (130°C). If the white chocolate isn't already in small chunks or fèves, chop it coarsely. Scatter it on a clean, dry rimmed baking sheet.

2 Roast the chocolate in the oven for about 45 minutes, stirring and smearing it around with a spatula every 5 to 10 minutes (make sure the spatula is clean and dry when you start each time). Don't worry if it looks lumpy and crumbly at times—it will smooth out as you stir (see photos on pages 232–33).

3 Continue cooking until the chocolate is as dark as you like (I like a rich toffee color). Stir in sea salt to taste.

4 Pour into a jar to store—it will harden as it cools, and may look mottled (this is normal for untempered chocolate). Store at room temperature, and warm it over a pot of barely simmering water when you're ready to use it. It should keep for several months.

---

## One-Ingredient Sweet Potato Caramel

### ADAPTED FROM BRAD LEONE

You can turn sweet potatoes into an earthy caramel without any added sugar (or added anything). This recipe makes ¼ cup of caramel, but scales up well.

Bake about 3 pounds (1.4kg) of sweet potatoes, peeled and chopped, with ½ cup water (120ml) in a 9 by 13-inch (23 by 33cm) baking dish, covered with foil, at 425°F (220°C) for an hour. Remove the foil and bake for 15 minutes more. Add another ½ cup (120ml) of water and scrape up any bits stuck to the baking dish.

Set a strainer lined with clean cheesecloth or a kitchen towel over a saucepan and pour the sweet potatoes (and any liquid) in. Once cool enough to handle, wring and squeeze as much liquid out from the potatoes as possible. (Save the leftover sweet potato mash to eat!)

Simmer the strained liquid for 15 to 20 minutes, until it starts to thicken and form a caramel, stirring often at the end. Pour into a jar and store in the refrigerator for up to 2 weeks.

To serve, warm up and loosen with butter or water as needed and salt to taste, if you like. Pour over ginger cake (page 226) or ice cream or chocolate desserts, or serve with savory dishes like roast meats or cheese plates.

# Brown Butter Tart Crust

## FROM PAULE CAILLAT

Sometimes it's nice to take it easy with our pastry, skip a few of the more traditionally grueling steps, and still end up with a tart. And there isn't a more easy-going pastry dough than this family recipe from Paule Caillat, founder of the Promenades Gourmandes Cooking School in Paris.

You don't have to roll it out or wait for it to chill, so you can go from "Hm, tart sounds good" to finished crust in about 40 minutes—no matter how cramped or humid your kitchen might be. Instead, all you do is brown butter, plus small but crucial amounts of oil, water, sugar, and salt, then quickly stir flour in. It sizzles and foams angrily for a moment, then settles into a rich, malleable sludge. Once the dough is cool enough to handle, you can press it into a tart pan and bake it straightaway.

The finished tart shell is crumbly and sandy, like a good shortbread, with that barely sweet, haunting quality that brown butter always brings to the table. It's also inexplicably flaky: You haven't laid the groundwork for those layers, which normally require you to cut pockets of icy butter into flour, but there they are.

Slick it with chocolate ganache, sweetened mascarpone, or, as pictured, lemon curd (page 236). And if you find yourself missing the demands of pastry-making, apply yourself to lining up concentric rings of berries across the top.

**Makes 1 (8½-inch/21cm) tart shell**

6 tablespoons (90g) unsalted butter, preferably a higher-fat European-style butter like Plugra

1 tablespoon vegetable oil

3 tablespoons water

1 tablespoon sugar (for savory fillings, just use 1 teaspoon)

Pinch of salt

All-purpose flour as necessary (about 5 ounces/150g or a slightly mounded cupful)

1 Preheat the oven to 410°F (210°C).

2 In a Pyrex-type oven-safe bowl, combine the butter, oil, water, sugar, and salt. Place in the hot oven for approximately 15 minutes, until the mixture is boiling and the butter starts browning. Remove from the oven, add the flour, and stir it in quickly. Keep adding flour, one spoonful at the time, until it pulls off the sides of the bowl and forms a ball.

3 Once the dough is cool enough to touch, press it into an 8½-inch (21cm) tart mold evenly with your fingertips. Pierce the bottom with a fork, and press the sides with the back of the fork to form ridges. Bake for 15 minutes, or until the crust is light brown and shows fine cracks.

4 Remove carefully from the oven. It is ready for filling—for example, with eggless lemon curd (page 236).

---

**GENIUS TIP**

The crust will crack less with European-style butter like Plugra, which has a slightly lower water (and higher fat) content than typical American butter, but blogger David Lebovitz recommends a brilliant patching technique for those cracks anyway: Just reserve a small knob of dough to spackle into any cracks after baking. (No need to bake again.)

"These two ladies, Mémé and Tante Léo, [my husband's grandmother and her sister,] never left France in their entire life, and now their recipe is repeated all over the world. I like this idea." —P.C.

# Eggless Lemon Curd

## FROM ELIZABETH FALKNER

The beauty of pastry chef Elizabeth Falkner's lemon curd is that, by taking eggs out of the picture, the curd is more forgiving and stable and can be served at any temperature—even warm—without risk of curdling. As with Jeni Britton Bauer's eggless ice cream technique (page 213), you also taste the lemon more clearly, without a filter of egg yolk.

**Makes about 2¼ cups (530ml)**

2 teaspoons lemon zest strips, about ⅛ inch (3mm) wide (from about 1 lemon)

¾ cup (150g) sugar

¾ cup (180ml) fresh lemon juice (from 4 to 5 lemons)

½ cup (115g) unsalted butter, cut into 1-inch (2.5cm) chunks

2 tablespoons agar agar flakes or powder (see Genius Tip)

½ cup (120ml) sweetened condensed milk

1 Place the lemon zest on a cutting board and mound 1 teaspoon of the sugar on top. Cut the zest and sugar together with a knife, alternately chopping and rubbing the mixture with the flat side of the knife. Gradually the mixture will transform into a smooth paste.

2 In a 2-quart (1.9L) or larger saucepan, combine the zest paste, remaining sugar, lemon juice, butter, and agar agar. Bring to a boil over medium heat, whisking continuously and taking care to get into the edges of the pan bottom with your whisk. After 4 to 5 minutes, reduce the heat to medium-low and simmer for 2 to 3 minutes, until you are sure the agar agar is dissolved. Pour the mixture into a heatproof bowl, whisk in the sweetened condensed milk, and let cool at room temperature for 10 to 15 minutes. Cover and refrigerate for at least 2 hours, but preferably overnight. It will keep in the refrigerator for up to 1 week.

### GENIUS TIP

Agar agar is a handy thickening agent derived from algae, and a vegan alternative to gelatin. Different brands can vary in their thickening power, but if your curd comes out too thick, simply rewarm it and whisk in a little water.

## Whipped Cream

### ADAPTED FROM NANCY SILVERTON

A simple trick that frees us to whip cream hours before dessert without worrying that it will deflate also wins big points for taste. Pastry chef Nancy Silverton mixes in a modest scoop of crème fraîche, about ¼ cup (60ml) to every 1 cup (240ml) of heavy cream. The crème fraîche breathes tang and depth into plain whipped cream, and the extra butterfat makes it more resilient, too.

Whip cold, cold cream by hand or with a mixer—just be sure to stop the moment you start to see soft peaks, then fold or gently whisk in the crème fraîche. If making ahead, underwhip the cream slightly and store, covered, in the refrigerator. Whisk briefly just before serving to restore its smoothness.

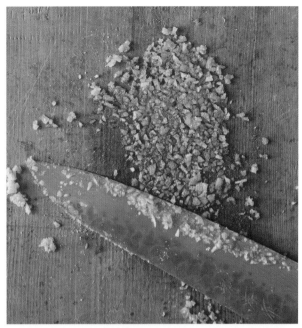

# Orange & Almond Cake

## FROM CLAUDIA RODEN

When you see that you have to boil oranges for 2 hours to make this recipe from Middle Eastern cookbook author Claudia Roden, you may be tempted to thumb to another cake, but I implore you to stay put.

When you boil oranges for that long, their bitterness slips into the water, so you can take advantage of the whole orange, thick spongy pith and all. The cooking is entirely hands-off once the oranges and water are in the pot, and makes your house smell like a holiday market. After 2 hours, taste some softened pith—it's creamy and citrusy and, for once, edible. (I tasted the water for you; it took up all that bitterness.)

When you blend your soft, chastened oranges in a food processor with a handful of other ingredients, you get a creamy, gluten-free, dairy-free batter. After it bakes in an unusually hot oven for a good hour, you get a cake that browns at the edges but looks like something between a tres leches cake and an Orange Julius on the inside. It sets up just barely, staying so puddinglike that, when you cut into it, if you haven't read this far, you will think you screwed something up. You didn't. Serve it with whipped cream (page 236) and tea.

---

"These cakes, which are half pudding, half cakes, can never fail. If they are undercooked they make a fine dessert with cream. They are too moist to ever be overcooked or to dry up." —C.R.

### Serves 6 to 10

2 large oranges
6 large eggs
2 cups plus 2 tablespoons (225g) ground almonds
1 cup plus 1 tablespoon (225g) sugar
1 teaspoon baking powder
Butter or oil, for the pan
Flour or more ground almonds, for the pan

1 Wash and boil the oranges (unpeeled) in a little water for nearly 2 hours (or for 30 minutes in a pressure cooker). Let them cool, then cut them open and remove the seeds. Turn the oranges into pulp by rubbing them through a sieve or by putting them in an electric blender or food processor.

2 Preheat the oven to 400°F (200°C). Butter and flour a cake pan with a removable base, if possible. (I used a 9 by 3-inch/23 by 7.5cm round cake pan, and you can use oil and almond flour if you're going for dairy-free and gluten-free.)

3 Beat the eggs in a large bowl. Add the ground almonds, sugar, baking powder, and orange puree and mix thoroughly. Pour into the prepared cake pan and bake for about 1 hour, then have a look at it—this type of cake will not go any flatter if the oven door is opened. If it is still very wet, leave it in the oven for a little longer. Cool in the pan before turning out.

# Acknowledgments

This book was crowd-sourced, in more ways than one—it would never have happened if not for the support of many people in widening circles around me.

Thank you:

To the geniuses whose recipes appear in this book and on Food52.

To the Food52 community members, staffers, and friends who sent in tips—see page 241 for the ones whose suggestions are in the book.

To Amanda Hesser and Merrill Stubbs for being my mentors, supporters, and friends since I hitched my wagon to theirs, and for letting me spend most of my time hunting these gems.

To the talented James Ransom for endless patience and the best photos in food.

To my assistant, Emily Stephenson, for devoting her Saturdays and more to helping me vet more recipes for the book, for tracking down permissions and quotes, and whose knowledge of vegetarian cookbooks helped balance out my own of meat and refined sugar.

To my brother, Billy Miglore, for cooking with me and quietly having my back, for casting a semi-unbiased eye on the text, and for carrying both a turkey and an iron to my last photo shoot and complaining about it only once.

To my parents, Allen and Susan Miglore, for showing me early on that food is worth caring about, and for teaching me how to cook.

To Mike Dunkley for listening, and eating, and grating cheese for the recipes, and frying eggs for dinner.

To Brette Warshaw for being my right hand, editor, tipster, and cheerleader.

To Food52's editorial team, my colleagues and friends whose talent and energy astonish me: Kenzi Wilbur, Marian Bull, Sarah Jampel, and Catherine Lamb. They carried me while I produced this book. Special thanks to Kenzi and Marian for their help with words.

To Jennifer Vogliano and Allison Buford for volunteering on less than a week's notice to cook at back-to-back weekends of photo shoots, making much of the beautiful food in this book. To Food52's head recipe tester Stephanie Bourgeois, for organizing retesting and consulting on baking genius. To Kristy Mucci, for staying up past her bedtime to test recipes with me, and being my partner in figuring out how to make food look good without faking it. To Henry Street Studio and Jono Pandolfi for lending their handsome ceramics for photoshoots for the book. To the many interns and editors, past and present, who've helped support the empire of Genius Recipes along the way—I would have sunk without you.

To my family, and friends who are like family, for never questioning why I would want to leave economics for food, and for listening to me talk about other people's recipes ever since: especially Grace Cowan and the whole Cowan family, the whole Miglore family, Hillary Krutzsch and Angela Fong, Stephanie Hair, Lauren Custer Dowling, Jasmine Dickison, Drew Mackie, Sarah Miller, and Anita Shepherd.

To my food friends and advocates, for inspiring, advising, and spreading the word: Charlotte Druckman, Lauren Shockey, Maddy Martin, Leah Koenig, Bryce Longton, Tien Nguyen, Gena Hamshaw, Chris Steighner, Kristin Donnelly, Susan Choung, Ben Mims, Sherry Rujikarn, Carey Yorio, Lori Galvin, Molly Wizenberg, Rozanne Gold, Peter Kaminsky, Alice Medrich, Nicholas Day, Rose Levy Beranbaum, Harold McGee, Shirley Corriher, Nathan Myhrvold, J. Kenji López-Alt, Roy Finamore, Francis Lam, and Molly O'Neill.

To the brilliant team at Ten Speed Press for their guidance and wisdom, and for helping us stay true to the vision of Food52 and Genius Recipes, the column: Aaron Wehner, Hannah Rahill, and Emma Campion, and especially my editor, Ali Slagle, for record email response times and for steering me through the challenges of translating a weekly column into a cookbook.

# Genius Tipsters

*These are the names, some real and some Food52 avatars, of people who shared tips that wound up in this book. Thank you all, and thanks to the many others who send in recipes and stories every week. Genius Recipes wouldn't be nearly as good, or as fun, without you.*

Africancook

Alexandra Stafford

Ali Slagle

Alice Medrich

Amanda Hesser

Ameliorator

Anna Hezel

April McGreger

Billy Miglore

breadwhisperer

Brette Warshaw

Bruce Cole of
    Edible SF

Cade

Caitlin Freeman

cheese1227

China Millman

cookbookchick

cookinginvictoria

creamtea

drbabs

ejm

Emily Stephenson

EmilyC

Evan Kleiman

Fairmount_market

fiveandspice

Francesca Gilberti

Frank Ball

hardlikearmour

Indrani Sen

J David B

JadeTree

jbban

JessicaBakes

Joy Huang

Judy Hesser

Kenzi Wilbur

Kristen Earle

Kristy Mucci

Lauren Shockey

Lennie Bennett

LL Stone

Maddy Martin

mainecook61

Marian Bull

Marisa Robertson-Textor

Matt Sartwell

Merrill Stubbs

mikeficus

MS

nancy o

nogaga

Nozlee Samadzadeh

Panfusine

Peter Kaminsky

Posie Harwood

Rachel Zarrow

Rhonda35

Rivka

shovel2spoon

Simran and Stacie at
    A Little Yumminess

Stephanie Bourgeois

Tom Hirschfeld

vivanat

vvvanessa

Will Levitt

# Credits

*Grateful acknowledgment is made to the following recipe creators and publishers for permission to reprint material. In addition to these credits, below you'll also find original sources that inspired the mini recipes throughout the book. Thank you to all.*

Nate Appleman and Shelley Lindgren: "Cheese Brodo" adapted from *A16* (Ten Speed Press), copyright © 2008 by D.O.C. Restaurant Group, LLC.

Dan Barber: "Cauliflower Steaks" from Blue Hill at Stone Barns, 2013. Recipe courtesy of the author.

Dan Barber: "One-Ingredient Whole Grain Crackers," adapted from Blue Hill at Stone Barns, 2012.

Jeni Britton Bauer: "Sweet Corn & Black Raspberry Ice Cream" from *Jeni's Splendid Ice Creams at Home*, copyright © 2011 by Jeni's Splendid Ice Creams, LLC. Used by permission of Artisan, a division of Workman Publishing Co., Inc., New York. All rights reserved.

Rose Levy Beranbaum: "Fresh Blueberry Pie" from *The Pie and Pastry Bible*, copyright © 1998 by Cordon Rose, Inc. Reprinted with the permission of Scribner Publishing Group, a division of Simon & Schuster, Inc. All rights reserved.

Peter Berley: "Balsamic Glazed Beets and Greens" from *The Modern Vegetarian Kitchen* by Peter Berley with Melissa Clark, copyright © 2000 by Peter Berley. Reprinted by permission of HarperCollins Publishers.

Paul Bertolli: "Cauliflower Soup" from *Cooking by Hand*, copyright © 2003 by Paul Bertolli. Used by permission of Clarkson Potter/Publishers, an imprint of the Crown Publishing Group, a division of Random House LLC. All rights reserved.

April Bloomfield and JJ Goode. "English Porridge" from *A Girl and Her Pig* (Ecco Press), copyright © 2012 by April Bloomfield. Reprinted by permission of HarperCollins Publishers.

Kim Boyce: "Whole Wheat Chocolate Chip Cookies" from *Good to the Grain* (Stewart, Tabori and Chang), copyright © 2010 by Kim Boyce. Reprinted with permission.

Alton Brown: "Baked Brown Rice," adapted from *Food Network*, 2005.

Marian Burros: "Purple Plum Torte" from *The Essential New York Times Cookbook*, edited by Amanda Hesser. Copyright © 2010 by The New York Times Company and Amanda Hesser. Used by permission of W. W. Norton & Company, Inc.

Paule Caillat: "Brown Butter Tart Crust" from Promenades Gourmandes, 2011. Recipe courtesy of the author.

Mario Carbone and and Rich Torrisi. "Spicy Sauce," adapted from Torrisi Italian Specialties and *New York Magazine*, 2012.

Penelope Casas: "Garlic Green Beans (*Judias verdes con ajo*)" from *The Foods and Wines of Spain*, copyright © 1982 by Penelope Casas. Used by permission of Alfred A. Knopf, an imprint of the Knopf Doubleday Publishing Group, a division of Random House LLC. All rights reserved.

David Chang and Peter Meehan: "Roasted Brussels Sprouts with Fish Sauce Vinaigrette" from *Momofuku*, copyright © 2009 by David Chang and Peter Meehan. Used by permission of Clarkson Potter/Publishers, an imprint of the Crown Publishing Group, a division of Random House LLC. All rights reserved.

Julia Child: "Tian de Courgettes au Riz" from *Mastering the Art of French Cooking, Volume 2* by Julia Child, with Louisette Bertholle and Simone Beck, copyright © 1970 by Alfred A. Knopf, a division of Random House LLC. Used by permission of Alfred A. Knopf, an imprint of the Knopf Doubleday Publishing Group, a division of Random House LLC. All rights reserved.

Melissa Clark: "Spiced Braised Lentils and Tomatoes with Toasted Coconut" from *Cook This Now* (Hyperion Books), copyright © 2011 by Melissa Clark. Used by permission of Hachette Books.

Sam and Sam Clark: "Warm Squash & Chickpea Salad with Tahini" from *Casa Moro* (Ebury), copyright © 2011 by Sam and Sam Clark. Reprinted by permission of The Random House Group Limited.

Tom Colicchio: "Chicken Stock," adapted from *Craft of Cooking* (Clarkson Potter), copyright © 2003 by TC Enterprises.

Shirley Corriher: "Touch-of-Grace Biscuits" from *Bakewise*, copyright © 2008 by Confident Cooking, Inc. Reprinted with the permission of Scribner Publishing Group, a division of Simon & Schuster, Inc. All rights reserved.

Marion Cunningham: "Raised Waffles" from *Breakfast Book*, copyright © 1987 by Marion Cunningham. Used by permission of Alfred A. Knopf, an imprint of the Knopf Doubleday Publishing Group, a division of Random House LLC. All rights reserved.

Nekisia Davis: "Olive Oil and Maple Granola" from Early Bird Foods & Co., LLC., 2012. Recipe courtesy of the author.

Faith Durand: "One-Ingredient Banana Ice Cream," adapted from *The Kitchn*, May 2011.

John T. Edge: "Cheater Soft Serve," adapted from *The Truck Food Cookbook* (Workman Publishing), copyright © 2012 by John T. Edge.

Frank Falcinelli, Frank Castronovo, and Peter Meehan: "Romaine Hearts with Caesar Salad Dressing" from *The Frankies Spuntino Kitchen Companion & Cooking Manual*, copyright © 2010 by Frank Falcinelli, Frank Castronovo, and Peter Meehan. Used by permission of Artisan, a division of Workman Publishing Co., Inc., New York. All rights reserved.

Elizabeth Falkner: "Eggless Lemon Curd" from *Elizabeth Falkner's Demolition Desserts*, copyright © 2007 by Elizabeth Falkner. Used by permission of Ten Speed Press, an imprint of the Crown Publishing Group, a division of Random House LLC. All rights reserved.

Caroline Fidanza: "Ship's Biscuit" from *Saltie*, copyright © 2012 by Caroline Fidanza. Used with permission of Chronicle Books LLC, San Francisco. Visit ChronicleBooks.com.

Roy Finamore: "Broccoli Cooked Forever" from *Tasty*, copyright © 2006 by Roy Finamore. Reprinted by permission of Houghton Mifflin Harcourt Publishing Company. All rights reserved.

Larry Forgione: "Strawberry Shortcakes" from *An American Place* (William Morrow and Company), copyright © 1996 by Larry Forgione. Recipe courtesy of the author.

Meta Given: "Pumpkin Pie" from *Meta Given's Modern Encyclopedia of Cooking* (J.G. Ferguson Publishing Company), copyright © 1969 by Meta Given.

Dorie Greenspan: "Marie-Hélène's Apple Cake" from *Around My French Table*, copyright © 2010 by Dorie Greenspan. Reprinted by permission of Houghton Mifflin Harcourt Publishing Company. All rights reserved.

José Pizarro: "Salt-Crusted Potatoes with Cilantro Mojo" from *Spanish Flavors*, copyright © 2013 by José Pizarro. Used by permission of Kyle Books.

Steven Raichlen: "Salt-Crusted Beef Tenderloin Grilled in Cloth (*Lomo al Trapo*)" from *Planet Barbecue!*, copyright © 2010 by Steven Raichlen. Used by permission of Workman Publishing Co., Inc., New York. All rights reserved.

Andrea Reusing: "Kale Panini" from *Cooking in the Moment*, copyright © 2011 by Andrea Reusing. Used by permission of Clarkson Potter/ Publishers, an imprint of the Crown Publishing Group, a division of Random House LLC. All rights reserved.

Michel Richard: "Onion Carbonara" from *Happy in the Kitchen*, copyright © 2006 by Michel Richard. Used by permission of Artisan, a division of Workman Publishing Co., Inc., New York. All rights reserved.

Eric Ripert and Christine Muhlke: "Crispy-Skinned Fish," adapted from *On the Line* (Artisan), copyright © 2008 by Eric Ripert. Recipe courtesy of the author.

Claudia Roden: "Orange and Almond Cake" from *Everything Tastes Better Outdoors*, copyright © 1981, 1984 by Claudia Roden. Used by permission of Alfred A. Knopf, an imprint of the Knopf Doubleday Publishing Group, a division of Random House LLC. All rights reserved.

Judy Rodgers: "Roasted Applesauce" from *The Zuni Cafe Cookbook*, copyright © 2002 by Judy Rodgers. Used by permission of W.W. Norton & Company, Inc.

Ruth Rogers and Rose Gray: "Strawberry Lemon Sorbet" from *The River Cafe Cookbook*, copyright © 1996 by Ruth Rogers and Rose Gray. Reprinted by permission of Ruth Rogers and Ebury Press.

Julee Rosso and Sheila Lukins: "Molasses Cookies" from *The Silver Palate Cookbook*, copyright © 2007 by Julee Rosso and Sheila Lukins. Used by permission of Workman Publishing Co., Inc., New York. All rights reserved.

Michael Ruhlman: "Rosemary-Brined, Buttermilk Fried Chicken" from *Ruhlman's Twenty*, copyright © 2011 by Michael Ruhlman. Used with permission of Chronicle Books LLC, San Francisco. Visit ChronicleBooks.com.

Roberto Santibañez and JJ Goode: "Classic Guacamole" from *Truly Mexican*. Copyright © 2011 by Roberto Santibañez. Reprinted by permission of Houghton Mifflin Harcourt Publishing Company. All rights reserved.

Cory Schreiber: "Herbed Salmon Baked on Rock Salt with Herb-Onion Caper Vinaigrette" from *Wildwood*, copyright © 2000 by Cory Schreiber. Used by permission of Ten Speed Press, an imprint of the Crown Publishing Group, a division of Random House LLC. All rights reserved.

Louisa Shafia: "Watermelon, Mint, and Cider Vinegar Tonic" from *The New Persian Kitchen*, copyright © 2013 by Louisa Shafia. Used by permission of Ten Speed Press, an imprint of the Crown Publishing Group, a division of Random House LLC. All rights reserved.

Alon Shaya: "Whole Roasted Cauliflower with Whipped Goat Cheese" from *Bon Appétit* magazine, May 2013. Reprinted with permission.

Kenny Shopsin: "Crepes" from *Eat Me*, copyright © 2008 by Kenny Shopsin. Used by permission of Alfred A. Knopf, an imprint of the Knopf Doubleday Publishing Group, a division of Random House LLC. All rights reserved.

Nancy Silverton: "Whipped Cream," adapted from *The Food of Campanile* (Villard), copyright © 1997 by Mark Peel.

Robert Simonson: "Cliff Old-Fashioned" from *The Old-Fashioned*, text copyright © 2014 by Robert Simonson. Used by permission of Ten Speed Press, an imprint of the Crown Publishing Group, a division of Random House LLC. All rights reserved.

Sitka & Spruce: "Yogurt with Toasted Quinoa, Dates, and Almonds," adapted by Amanda Hesser, 2012.

Nigel Slater: "Chocolate Muscovado Banana Cake" from *Notes from the Larder*, text copyright © 2012 by Nigel Slater. Used by permission of Ten Speed Press, an imprint of the Crown Publishing Group, a division of Random House LLC. All rights reserved.

Bill Smith: "Green Peach Salad," from *Seasoned in the South*, copyright © 2005 by Bill Smith. Used by permission of Algonquin, a division of Workman Publishing Co., Inc., New York. All rights reserved.

Molly Stevens: "Ginger Juice," adapted from *All About Roasting* (W. W. Norton & Company), copyright © 2011 by Molly Stevens.

Heidi Swanson: "Chickpea Stew" from *Super Natural Every Day*, copyright © 2011 by Heidi Swanson. Used by permission of Ten Speed Press, an imprint of the Crown Publishing Group, a division of Random House LLC. All rights reserved.

Hervé This: "Chocolate Mousse" from *Molecular Gastronomy* (Columbia University Press), copyright © 2002 by Columbia University Press. Reprinted with permission of the publisher.

Sylvia Thompson: "Fresh Ginger Cake" from *Feasts and Friends* (North Point Press), copyright © 1988 by Sylvia Thompson. Recipe courtesy of the author.

Todd Thrasher: "Tomato Water Bloody Mary," Restaurant Eve, 2014. Recipe courtesy of the author.

Valrhona: "Caramelized White Chocolate" from L'Ecole du Grand Chocolat, copyright © 2013 by Valrhona USA.

Roger Vergé: "Fried Eggs with Wine Vinegar" from *Cuisine of the Sun* (Macmillan), copyright © 1979 by Roger Vergé.

Anya Von Bremzen: "Potato Soup with Fried Almonds" from *The New Spanish Table*, copyright © 2005 by Anya Von Bremzen. Used by permission of Workman Publishing Co., Inc., New York. All rights reserved.

Jean-Georges Vongerichten and Mark Bittman: "Ginger Fried Rice," adapted from the *New York Times*, January 27, 2010.

Alice Waters: "Ratatouille" from *The Art of Simple Food*, copyright © 2007 by Alice Waters. Used by permission of Clarkson Potter/ Publishers, an imprint of the Crown Publishing Group, a division of Random House LLC. All rights reserved.

Nach Waxman: "Brisket of Beef" from *The New Basics Cookbook*, copyright © 1989 by Julee Rosso and Sheila Lukins. Used by permission of Workman Publishing Co., Inc., New York. All rights reserved.

Patricia Wells: "Green Lentil Salad" from *Bistro Cooking*, copyright © 1989 by Patricia Wells. Used by permission of Workman Publishing Co., Inc., New York. All rights reserved.

Patricia Wells: "Lemon Salt," adapted from *Salad as a Meal* (William Morrow and Company), copyright © 2011 by Patricia Wells.

Anne Willan and Mark Cherniavsky: "Spiced Red Wine (*Ypocras*)" from *The Cookbook Library*, copyright © 2012 by The Regents of the University of California. Reproduced with permission of University of California Press via Copyright Clearance Center.

Virginia Willis: "Deviled Eggs" from *Bon Appetit, Y'all*, copyright © 2008 by Virginia Willis. Used by permission of Ten Speed Press, an imprint of the Crown Publishing Group, a division of Random House LLC. All rights reserved.

Paula Wolfert: "Herb Jam with Olives and Lemon" from *The Slow Mediterranean Kitchen*, copyright © 2003 by Paula Wolfert. Reprinted by permission of Houghton Mifflin Harcourt Publishing Company. All rights reserved.

Whitney Wright: "One-Ingredient Corn Butter," adapted from *Gilt Taste*, 2012.

# Index

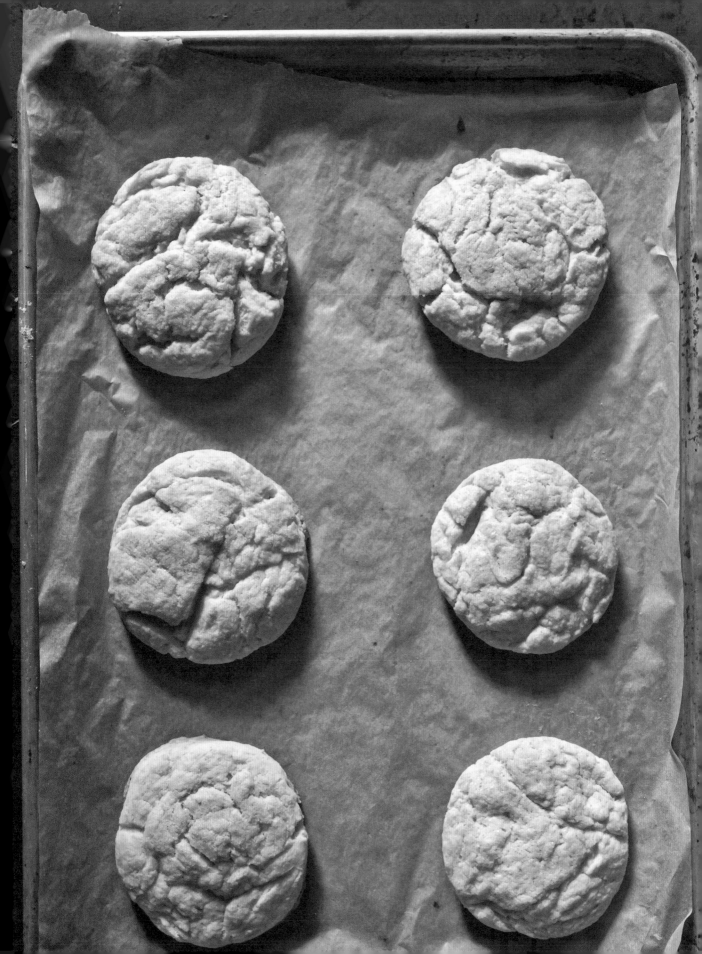

Published in the United States by Ten Speed Press, an imprint
of the Crown Publishing Group, a division of Random House
LLC, a Penguin Random House Company, New York.
www.crownpublishing.com
www.tenspeed.com

Ten Speed Press and the Ten Speed Press colophon are
registered trademarks of Random House LLC.

Permissions information can be found on pages 243–45.

Library of Congress Cataloging-in-Publication Data
Miglore, Kristen.
Food52 genius recipes: 100 recipes that will change the way you
cook / Kristen Miglore; photography by James Ransom.
 pages cm
1. Cooking. I. Food52. II. Title. III. Title: Genius recipes.
TX714.M535 2015
641.5—dc23
2014034413

Hardcover ISBN: 978-1-60774-797-0
eBook ISBN: 978-1-60774-798-7

Printed in China
Design by Emma Campion

10 9 8 7 6 5 4 3 2 1

First Edition